METHODOLOGY HANDBOOK FOR INFORMATION MANAGERS

METHODOLOGY HANDBOOK FOR INFORMATION MANAGERS

ALL YOU EVER WANTED TO KNOW ABOUT
METHODOLOGY BUT WERE AFRAID TO ASK

Simon Holloway

Gower Technical

Aldershot · Brookfield USA · Hong Kong · Singapore · Sydney

Published by
Gower Technical
Gower House,
Croft Road,
Aldershot,
Hants GU11 3HR
England

Gower Publishing Company,
Old Post Road,
Brookfield,
Vermont 05036
U.S.A.

Electronically typeset using Aldus PageMaker in 14pt and 12pt Palatino on an Apple Mackintosh SE by Simon Holloway

ISBN 0 566 09023 6

Printed and bound in Great Britain by
Anchor Press Ltd, Tiptree, Essex

CONTENTS

APPENDICES

ILLUSTRATIONS

Figures

PREFACE

During my time, both as a database administrator and as a consultant, I have become aware that data processing management have a problem in understanding the terminology that is used in new technology and techniques. This is an outcome of the era, when data processing personnel were not sent on training courses to learn new skills, but had to learn them "on the job". Many current data processing managers have grown up through the ranks; having been programmers and then analysts. The data processing education industry has done a lot to provide training for the lower levels, but there is very little at the managerial level to give these people an overview of current technology and techniques. What is on offer, are a number of half day product seminars from vendors.

This book is intended to fulfill this gap, by providing an overview of one particular area - methodology. A lot has been said and written about methodologies in recent years. The subject has become more important, particularly with the adoption by the UK government of a particular methodology. Readers are invited to dip into particular chapters that are of interest.

The book starts with an introduction as to what is a methodology and how to select one. The second chapter analyses the current marketplace in the UK and gives a brief overview of four current methodologies. Chapters three to eleven describe various techniques that are used in methodologies. At the end of each chapter are suggestions for further reading. The final chapter looks at the impact of fourth generation software and techniques on the current organisational structure, not just for data processing, but also how the end user is affected.

I would like to thank all the people who have helped me gain the knowledge about methodologies over the years, either through reading their articles or books, or through listening to them speak. This book would not have happened if I had not got the support of my wife - Susan. Especial thanks are due to her for the stream of cups of tea and putting up with my disappearance to the study to write the book.

Simon Holloway
Berkhamsted
July 28th 1988

1. METHODOLOGY

1.1 APPLICATION BACKLOG

Although we now have a variety of tried and proven tools and techniques for application system development, it can be said that we, as information systems developers, have failed. Baldock (1) summarises the problem as follows "..The rate at which software can be produced (which is a factor of the number of people available to do the work and their work output) has not kept pace....., contributing to an increase in the 'application backlog'".

Many large organisations have a 2 to 5 year application backlog. This backlog is not a large number of equal projects or tasks; it is a very diverse three-dimensional workload. The first dimension of the application backlog is different types of applications. They range all the way from large scale new systems to ad-hoc requests. At least 50% of the application backlog could be termed 'invisible'. That is applications that are needed to be developed, yet because end-users are still waiting for work to be finished by data processing, has not been made known to the latter. In addition to the variety of applications in the backlog, an examination of any one application will reveal that it requires a combination of program types in order to work. This is the second dimension to the application backlog. Applications are not 100% batch or 100% online, they are a combination of the two. The third dimension of the backlog is the traditional software life cycle.

Data Processing has to find a way of bridging this gap within the constraints placed upon them of people available, finance available and software available in the market place. The software industry has responded to the this requirement in a number of ways. But it is upto Data Processing management to sift through the hype and pick a set of tools and techniques that fit the philosophy of their organisation best.

1.2. TOOLS AND TECHNIQUES TO DEVELOP INFORMATION MANAGEMENT SYSTEMS

What has been done in the computer industry to help companies manage their data resource and develop effective information management systems? I see that there are 6 main facilities that have been provided:-

* Database Management Systems - to allow applications to share data

* Data Dictionary Systems - to allow automated control and documentation of the data

* Query Languages - to allow end-users direct access to the data resource

* 4th Generation Systems - to allow for more rapid application development

* System Development Methodologies - to allow for planned and controlled develop-

ment of information systems

- CASE Tools - to automate the database and systems design process

In the Nineties, no longer will we buy these tools and techniques separately, they will have become one integrated package for managing the information needs of an organisation. The database management system will have become less visible, whilst still remaining the bedrock. The data dictionary system will have become dynamic and also less visible; communication to it will be through design aid software. Methodologies will have become so tied up with the software, that I foresee a problem for independent consultancies, who have been the leaders in the field, unless they can persuade software vendors to adopt their methods.

Companies that will succeed in the Nineties will be those that pick the right combination of hardware, software and methods, in order to provide information to the right people at the right time with the appropriate level of security. These companies will also be the ones that recognise now, and start planning accordingly, that their organisation will need to change.

Distribution is certainly something that will be important. No longer are we talking about mainframe to mainframe or mainframe to mini. The birth of the PC and its ever increasing capacity mean that LAN's and PC to mainframe connections are of more importance.

1.3   METHODOLOGIES

The development of corporate databases and information systems written in 4th Generation environment products will be the most important DP activities for many years to come. The end-users demand for information as well as the requirements for efficient processing of traditional production systems has been increasing. In the last decade there have been a number of methodologies developed that purported to study the business as a whole and suggested a 'subject database' and information systems architecture to meet business needs.

The objectives of Information Systems can be summarised as follows:-

- Senior management commitment - Clear communication with senior management concerning the objectives and role of information systems in the organisation, and commitment to apply the appropriate resource once priorities have been set.

- A clear sense of direction - Agreement is needed on the main business goals and priorities, and on the information system needs and priorities which stem from them.

- Effective organisation - the information systems function must be organised so as to support growing needs such as end-user computing, data resource control and application architecture.

- A good overall development method - an effective approach to application development consists of more than just a good bunch of techniques.

- Appropriate levels of skill and resources - many good ideas founder due to lack of adequate skills and resources. Adequate planning so as to meet the demand is essential.

The above objectives would typically be transformed into an action plan which may have the following elements:-

- Identify and prioritise the business needs - based on analysis of the business plans, determine what information is needed now, and in the future to run the business.

- Assess current system coverage - Assess these needs in relation to the coverage achieved with current systems.

- Target efforts accurately to the business priorities - Adjust application development priorities and resource allocation so as to be most responsive to the business priorities.

- Build and maintain architecture - Establish clear overall architectures for applications and databases to act as a blueprint and control for subsequent development activity.

- Maximize user involvement, commitment and sponsorship - Ensure the users set and sponsor development priorities. If possible it is a good idea that they should be funding the development.

- Deliver business benefits incrementally - Small frequent deliveries are far more effective for gaining and retaining user confidence. Most applications can be phased so as to match this criteria.

- Plan the migration - Any target is only as good as the route followed to get there. Each step must be :

  * attractive and cost beneficial in business terms

  * resilient to nasty surprises in technology or business changes

  * a demonstrable contribution to the end result.

It is now possible to see what an overall application development method cover.

1.4   WHY IS A GOOD METHODOLOGY NECESSARY ?

It lessens the risk of wasting resources, and thus money, on system development. A proven methodology means that the most effective way of doing things is defined in advance of the project, so that at all times there is a framework for development staff.

In addition, it increases the productivity of development staff. A good methodology does this in a number of ways:

- By providing a standard framework so that the developer does not have to reinvest the wheel for each project.

- Like a good kit of tools, it provides the right tools to enable each development task to be successfully completed.

- It allows effective review procedures so that errors and inconsistencies can be identified early.

- It acts as a productivity aid by reducing the amount of development documentation.

A good system development methodology improves the quality of the systems finally developed. It forces the developer to produce flexible systems that are adequately documented as they are developed. In addition, it allows the analyst to identify accurately the needs of the user, as well as allowing the user to verify easily that his needs have been taken care of.

A methodology provides a management window for reviewing project progress. At each stage management has a check list for accessing what tasks should be completed and what deliverables are due.

Communications are improved as a methodology provides a communications base between all those concerned with system development:

- User and analyst

- Analyst and programmer

- Analysts and database administrator

- Data administrator and database administrator

- Staff and management

- Operations and the development team

Finally, it makes planning easier. If you cannot plan it, you cannot do it. A good methodology allows you to plan, monitor, correct and re-plan as the project progresses.

1.5 OBJECTIVES OF A METHODOLOGY

The objectives of a good methodology should be as follows :-

- Clear delineation between application oriented tasks and data oriented tasks, and those viewing data and applications together. *OBJECT ORIENTED ?*

- Separation of design from analysis, to provide flexible business and technology changes. *TIMESPAN?*

- Emphasis on a development strategy rather than on ad-hoc problem solving.

- Based on a development plan which allows for both user priorities and logical constraints.

- As great an effort is put into analysis of the business, as into the design and construction of computer systems.

- A clear distinction is made between user-oriented tasks, when full user involvement is expected, and technical tasks, when little user involvement is expected.

- Each stage in the life-cycle provides a firm and complete foundation for the next stage, while permitting iterations within each stage.

- Adaptable framework approach as described by British Computer Society Information Systems Analysis and Design Working Party (2) centered on the data dictionary.

- A high degree of prototyping, producing a working system specification without database design commitment and involving structured English documentation standards embodied in the data dictionary.

- Structured design techniques for both system and program design.

1.6   REQUIREMENTS FOR AN EFFECTIVE DEVELOPMENT METHODOLOGY

Tozer (3) states that an effective application development methodology should : -

- **Be Easy to Use** - The average analyst or programmer should be able to use it. All to often, the approaches advocated only work in the hands of those few who would probably build good systems with no methodology support at all.

- **Cover all Phases** - Application identification and development is typically divided into a number of phases. The number and the names differ as does the extent to which current methodologies address them. There follows a list of the phases that should be covered by any methodology. The phases are :-

    * **Planning** - Identification of business information needs and priorities, and their reflection in a portfolio of applications and databases needed by the company. Comparison with what exists, and the subsequent development of an overall plan for the upgrade of applications, equipment, skills and resources.

    * **Functional Requirements Definition** - For specific, high priority application areas, the in-depth analysis of the needs.

    * **External Design** - For each application subsystem, a definition of all aspects of the user interface and the processing rules.

    * **Internal Design** - Design of all technical aspects of the application, and its databases, taking account of performance, security and integrity and economic issues.

    * **Development** - Implementation of the system in the chosen media; including all aspects of integration and testing.

    * **Cut-Over** - Conversion of the application into the live operational mode.

    * **Maintenance** - Everything which happens to the application during the whole of its operational life.

- **Be Relevant to Classes of Application to be Developed** - There are many types of applications. The range of applications can be categorized in the following manner:-

    * **Transaction Processing System** - whose main characteristics are that they process relatively high volume routine business events of the company. They tend to be predefined and relatively simple in nature.

* **Routine Operational Control Systems** - which tend to carry out monitoring and exception reporting resulting from the previous type of systems.

* **Planning and Analysis Applications** - where there is a higher degree of volatility, and it is more likely that further ad hoc processes will be generated, resulting from the user's reaction to the previous answer. These applications tend to have lower processing volumes, with greater volatility of requirements. They tend to be more heavily dependent upon good presentational interfaces and require heavier computing power per request to support them.

* **Strategic Applications** - which may be of almost any type with any mixture or combination characteristics. Their inherent characteristics are that they are mostly concerned with external information. The user interface is highly critical to their success. The requirements for them are almost entirely unpredictable and extremely volatile.

All of the above features are of prime importance when choosing the particular methodology to be used. The following features, all aimed at increasing productivity, whilst maintaining system quality are equally important but not always recognised as such:-

• **Data/Process Technique Balance** - the selection criteria must be, a balance between short term project productivity and system quality. Any reasonable definition of quality must include ease of maintenance, fleixibility in the face of future enhancements and production of a system the user actually wants in terms of function and performance. All of these aspects of quality contribute to long term productivity by reducing the time spent in maintaining live systems. If these two techniques (data and process) are not balanced then discrepancies in design may not be noticed until later in development process and the later they are noticed the more costly they will be to correct. If a methodology is processed orientated, then it is likely that all the possible logical paths running through a process will be understood, allowing a specification of a logically complete process. If the methodology is data orientated, it will tend to promote a coherence and completeness of processes around a single data entity.

• **Quality of Documentation** - documentation should only be produced to facilitate a common understanding within the current project phase or to carry information necessary to a further phase within the development process. Substantial gains in productivity will be achieved by eliminating redundant documentation. The maxim " a good picture is worth a thousand words" is as relevant to the design of information systems as to any other communication process.

• **Vendor Support** - many companies have attempted to use many development techniques and create their own or their own versions of a development methodology. Most will tell you that whatever the package, vendor support in the form of training and consultancy, is vital to the effectiveness of its use.

- **Narrowing the Descriptive Gap** - Another method of achieving a gain in productivity is to narrow the gap between, the forms of system description intelligible to the business manager and the forms of system description usable by the systems designer. The latter can be narrowed by the use of 4th generation languages that employ standard logical constructs and avoid the need for complex database navigation.. The gap can also be narrowed for the business manager's end, starting with systems specification. Firstly the the overall structure of the system can be defined using graphical techniques, such as structure diagrams and data flow diagrams. Next the the inputs and outputs can be defined using prototyping techniques. This will not only allow the user to see what is actually going to be the end product, but also provides automatic production of associated documentation. The delivery of a system model that is vivid to the end user, should be one of the most important consequences of this process. Finally it is possible to describe the logical process necessary to move from input to output.

1.7   SELECTION CRITERIA FOR METHODOLOGIES

The Sixties was the decade when good approaches for designing computer systems were discovered. The roots of all structured programming and structured analysis and design methodologies have come from the discoveries made in that decade. Correspondingly, the Seventies were the decade of data analysis. Data Analysis is the approach of undertaking detailed analysis of the inherent data structures for an organisational area or system. It came to the fore and in some cases significantly overshadowed the functional analysis and design approaches which had hitherto gained sway. The Eighties has seen the birth of the "Framework" approach - methodologies that use a variety of techniques covering the whole development lifecycle. In 1984, the Information Systems and Analysis Working party of the BCS Database Specialist group produced a journal of development (2) discussing this framework approach. All of the methodologies that are part of this group have 2 ideas in common:-

- Recognition of a Strategic Planning phase linked to the business plans of the company.

- The splitting of data and functional analysis into separate phases with primary emphasis on data.

The criteria list below are those developed by myself (4), initially for a talk to MSc students at Kingston Polytechnic. They are ranked into two groups which reflect the relative importance and weighting to be ascribed to the criteria.

Primary Criteria

- Completeness - Do they cover all activities? Do they deal with all important aspects of each activity? The activities required by the method should be :-

  Information Resource Planning
  User Involvement
  Business modelling
  Structured Analysis and Design
  Prototyping
  Data Analysis using normalisation
  Data Modeling
  Structured Programming
  Structured Testing
  Interviewing Skills
  Implementation
  Project management and control

- Exploitation of the Software Products used by the organisation.

- Ease of learning and use for both DP and user staff. What education/training is available and what audience is it geared to ?

- Flexibility Do they cope with different sizes, types and complexities of systems?

- Supplier Profile Is the method readily available? What support will be provided? What documentation will be provided? What training will be offered? Who is using the method?

- Can they cope with changes during development of a system?

- Do they recognise the integration of data and processes?

- Do they fit into the structure of your company? Are they compatible with your systems and data architecture?

Secondary Criteria

- Do they avoid duplication of documentation/effort?

- Do they allow the use of automated tools and documentation aids?

- Do they help identify the boundary between User procedures and computer System transactions?

- Will the methods aid in on-line transaction design?

- Do they aid system maintainability?

- What effect do they have on project management?

- Can activities be overlapped?

- Are there built-in checks on completeness/correctness?

- Is the level of detail required defined for each activity?

- Is all the documentation necessary and relevant?

1.8 METHODOLOGY COMPONENTS

When an organisation buys a 4th Generation Environment and a Database Management System its most immediate concern is how to construct applications and how to implement a database. A methodology will help him do this. Figure 1.1 shows a methodology whose bottom layer (layer 1) assists in these two areas. If a methodology has only these two components it can be said that it facilitates the effective translation of an application design into the 4th Generation System programs and database design into working the Database Management System databases. It is obvious it is necessary to have application design and database design. This suggests that another layer is needed to help with design.

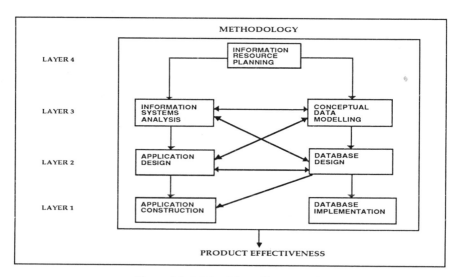

Figure 1.1 : Methodology Components

If a methodology has the application design and database design layer (layer 2), it can be said that it facilitates the effective translation of user requirements into the 4th Generation System programs and the Database Management System databases. This suggests that before design is started, it is necessary to understand user requirements. So the next higher layer (layer 3) helps identify and clarify user requirements.

Determining user requirements adds a layer to the methodology which consists of information systems analysis and conceptual data modeling. Information systems analysis considers the processes and the data used by the processes, by prototyping the requirements with the user. Conceptual data modeling is primarily to do with data structures. A methodology that consists of these first three layers fosters product effectiveness in supporting a functional area of business. One of the criteria of effectiveness is that the products support integrated applications of the business and share common data. Layer 3 of the methodology contributes to this goal. Conceptual data modeling contributes to the sharing of databases. However, the parts of the methodology that have been discussed so far, all have limited scope; they have the scope of an application project. To increase the likelihood of applications working well together and sharing data, a higher level planning activity is needed. This covers the whole of the company or a large part of it, and is called Information Resource Planning -IRP (layer 4). When a methodology has all 4 layers, it can be said that it fosters product effectiveness in supporting interrelated applications which share common data.

This last layer, layer 4, relies on input form Business Planning. IRP is shaped by Business Planning, in order that the product effectiveness supports the mission and goals of the company. Hence, the methodology will go along way towards increasing the business executive's and user's satisfaction with the products.

Figure 1.2 gives a more complete picture of the methodology. Project management is needed to monitor each part of the methodology. Data Administration ensures that projects adhere to the methodology and establishes and administers the company data policy. Database technical implementation of the data policy. Some companies have a separate organisational unit called an Information Centre. This supports end-user computing. The methodology provides the foundation for end-user computing. Application Testing and Implementation phases are also needed to complete the information engineering life cycle. Implementation includes the installation, maintenance and review of information systems.

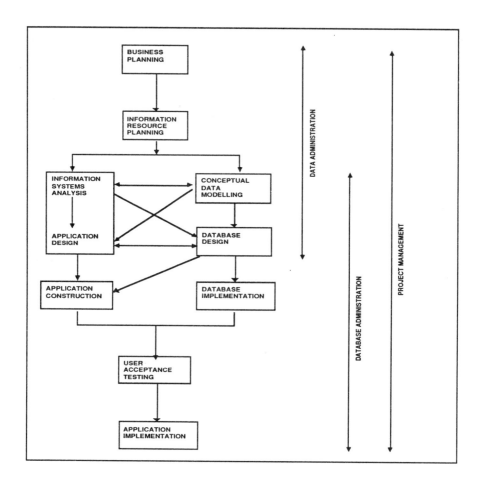

Figure 1.2 : Relational Information Systems Design - RISD

REFERENCES

1. INFORMATION SYSTEMS ANALYSIS AND DESIGN : WAYS OF ACCELERAT
    ING THE CYCLE AND BUILDING BETTER SYSTEMS, R.Baldock, State of the Art
    Report 12:3, Edited by E.E.Tozer, Pergmon Infotech Ltd.,1984.

2. INFORMATION SYSTEMS DEVELOPMENT : A FLEXIBLE FRAMEWORK, British
    Computer Society Information Systems and Design Working Party Journal of Devel
    opments, Editor R. Maddison, 1983-1984

3. A REVIEW OF CURRENT DATA ANALYSIS METHODOLOGIES, E. Tozer, Data Analysis In Practice, British Computer Society Database Specialist Group, 1985.

4. EVALUATION OF DATABASE MANAGEMENT SYSTEM : A QUESTION OF CHOICE, Simon Holloway, paper presented at Kingston Polytechnic, Feb.1987

2.   THE METHODOLOGY MARKETPLACE

2.1   THE EVOLUTION OF OFF-THE-SHELF METHODOLOGIES

When computer first appeared in the early Fifties, they were simple improvements on the of tabulating machines, that were programmed by connecting myriads of wires on a board. The next generation saw the writing of code consisting of a series of zeros and ones; this described the switching within the computer. These then evolved into tape and disk driven machines and languages such as Assembler and COBOL. During this evolution, application systems were designed and implemented by programmers (the coders) talking directly to the users. When I first became involved with computers in the early Seventies, this state of affairs had already fallen apart. On the one hand, business problems that were being computerised were more complex, whilst on the other hand, the technicalities of the computer in terms of both hardware and software had advanced.

Techniques for the analysis and design of systems to solve these complex issues were needed. To further complicate the issue, the advent of TP monitors and database management systems also brought in new problems. The Seventies and Eighties have seen the evolution of these techniques of analysis and design into packages of techniques, that are described as "methodologies". In addition, these years have seen the birth of the "off-the-shelf" methodology supplied in the main by consultancy houses, but also by some software vendors. These companies have been prepared to offer their packaging of techniques for analysis and design, which their own employees have been using in the field. In no country in the world, has this been more in evidence than in Great Britain. Today, you will find that there are a large number of suppliers of methodologies. Why are there so many separate methodologies? Tagg (1) has suggested that there is a parallel in the proliferation of religious sects:-

> "Despite the fact that they are 95% agreed in their aims and their broad areas
> of getting there, they nevertheless manage to stay separate. Each sect
> jealously guards its own style and magic ingredients."

In the last few years, the methodology market in Great Britain has undergone somewhat of a shake-up. Two distinct style or sects have risen to prominence. These are the Information Engineering sect and the SSADM sect.

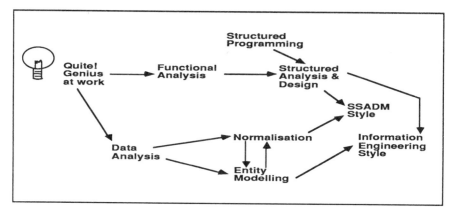

Figure 2.1 : The Evolution of Methodologies

2.1.1   The Information Engineering Sect

This sect is associated with the writings of the most well-known of the data processing gurus, James Martin. However the method has its foundations on the techniques evolved on both sides of the Atlantic; from ideas that Martin put forward in his books of the middle Seventies while working for IBM, and from the CACI methodology D2S2 developed in Great Britain in the Seventies. Although the term "Information Engineering" is used by Matin's company, James Martin Associates , as the name of their methodology, many other methodology vendors have been formed from the original nucleus of CACI consultants. The CACI methodology has a mnemonic of "D2S2", standing for "Development of Data Sharing Systems". Its main designer was Ian Palmer, with input from Geoffrey Baker (diagrammatic conventions), David Gradwell (classification technique) and Carl Rosen-quist (entity life cycles). CACI in the late seventies was the "powerhouse" of knowledge in database and system design. Almost all the foremost authorities in Great Britain on methodologies have come from CACI. Some of consultants left to join ICL and Database Consultants Europe during the late Seventies, taking with them the ideas of D2S2 and formulating them into slight deviants. In 1981, this "powerhouse" underwent a major upheaval with the breakaway of Palmer and a number of other senior consultants to form DMW , which later became James Martin Associates.

During the early 80's, CACI became the UK distributor of the ORACLE relational database management system. They set up a separate division to cope with this. In 1985, this division was hived off and ORACLE UK was formed as a separate company. The staff of the division went at the same time. Unfortunately for CACI, this included Richard Barker who had taken over the role of methodology developer from Palmer, and so was bourn SQL Design Methodology

Also during the early 80's, CACI started work on producing a product called SYSTEM FACTORY. This was CACI's response to help data processing respond to the application backlog and maintenance problem. In August 1984, work was stopped on the product by

CACI. A major portion of the consultants involved in this project in the UK left CACI and formed a new company - Inforem, and another deviant of the D2S2 methodology was bourn.

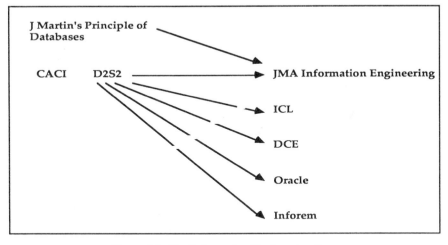

Figure 2.2 : The Information Engineering Sect.

All the methodologies in this sect have the following common principles :-

• they cover the whole of the life-cycle, from information resource planning through to implementation;

• they use the same underlying entity relationship diagramming representation;

• they have discreet sections, in which a set of particular techniques is used to produce a particular output required;

• they all have started to computerise their methods to some degree through the use of CASE tool.

2.1.2 The SSADM Sect

In 1980, the British Government body responsible for computer technology, the Central Computer and Telecommunications Agency (CCTA) put out to tender for vendors to provide a Structured Development Methodology to cover all aspects of systems analysis and design. Between May and November 1980, forty-seven different products from thirty five companies in the USA and Europe were evaluated. From this initial list a short list of five was produced. During December 1980, each of the short-listed vendors gave a presentation of its methodology, and described how it saw the plan for government acquisition. The contract was awarded to Learmouth and Burchett management Systems Limited (LBMS) in January 1981, and resulted in the development of "Structured Systems Analysis and Development Method "(SSADM).

Just like the Information Engineering sect, the SSADM sect has its foundations in another methodology, MODUS from BIS Applied Systems. MODUS was first formulated in 1965 as a comprehensive approach to systems development standards. Over the years, MODUS has taken on board new techniques such as Structured Programming from the ideas of Jackson, Structured Analysis from the ideas of Gane and Sarson, and Data Analysis from the ideas of both Codd and CACI. In 1977, two BIS consultants, Roger Learmouth and Rainer Burchett, left the company and formed their own company, Learmouth and Burchett Management Systems. Other companies have been formed by consultants from both organisations, such as Model Systems, who have developed slight variations on the basic approach.

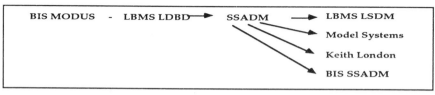

Figure 2.3 : The SSADM Sect

SSADM has been mandatory for all British Government information technology projects since 1983. The adoption of a methodology by the British Government has effected the methodology market in the country to a large degree. It has alerted many commercial data processing managers to the importance of methodologies. The CCTA launched a major drive to promote SSADM in commerce at the beginning of 1987. This came at the same time as the use of outside contractors on government project was increasing. The National Computing Centre (the NCC) were invited to provide the marketing expertise -, as well as helping to polish up the documentation, training and promotional work.

2.2.   UK METHODOLOGIES AND THEIR VENDORS

In the following sections, I have given an overview of these four methodologies and a profile of their vendors. The objective of this chapter is to provide the reader with a guide to these main methodologies and to highlight the major techniques that they use. These major techniques are then covered in more detail in the subsequent chapters.

2.3.   BUSINESS INTELLIGENCE SERVICES (BIS)

BIS was started by Brian Allison in 1964. It was set up initially to work in the areas of Market Research and Training. Services were offered initially to manufacturing and the pulp industry. The aim was to provide know how to managers baffled by new technology. The firm quickly moved into banking and used its financial experience as a platform for rapid and lucrative overseas expansion. The company has some 1,200 people employed.

The group is now organised into four main areas of business:

- Software - this has 2 major areas, BIS Software and BIS Insurance. They concentrate on products, like the flagship - MIDAS banking package, and the insurance packages - FOLIO and SOLAR.

- . Information Systems - BIS Applied Systems is probably the best known name in the group.. It deals with consultancy, training and methodology product (IPSE).

- Marketing - this group includes such names as Macintosh International, BIS-Shrapnel, BIS Market research and Informat.

- Direct Marketing - this is responsible for clients such as Prudential Assurance (UK's largest insurance company) and Ford UK.

The consultancy side covers areas such as strategy, and security, database and distributed systems, office automation and communications, the MODUS methodology and expert systems. In December 1986, it was announced that BIS had been acquired by the USA company NYNEX.

MODUS is a set of information system methods (2,3) which cover the aspects of information system management from general business planning through to maintenance. The techniques to be used during each phase have been developed to supplement rather than replace conventional good practice. They are designed so that they can be implemented a phase at a time or for the complete project framework. Figure 2.4 shows an activity summary of the methods that are used in MODUS.

2.3.1 Initiate Feasibility Study

Previous systems planning should have indicated the potential need for systems within a certain area of concern. This area is defined and terms of reference are created for a feasibility study. Prior planning may not have been carried out, perhaps because the area of concern has been identified by an ad hoc user request. In this case, a brief survey will usually be necessary prior to creating the terms of reference for the feasibility study. In some cases, the survey will indicate that systems development is not appropriate and no feasibility study will be started.

2.3.2 Study Feasibility

This is the first major project phase. Within it a study is made of the technical and economic feasibility of creating an information system within the area of concern. This is true whether the proposed development is a new system or the enhancement of an existing one.

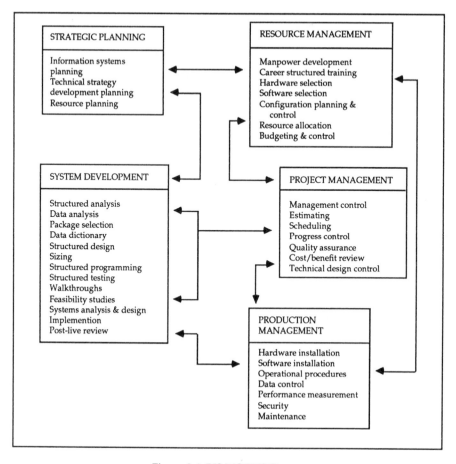

Figure 2.4 BIS MODUS Stages

During a feasibility study, sufficient analysis is carried out to gain an understanding of the existing system and the objectives which systems within the application area must fulfill. The requirements of a new system are defined in terms of facilities and information, together with broad performance targets. Various approaches are considered and outline designs produced in order to assess potential complexity, technical feasibility and likely development and operational costs. The most appropriate path for development is selected.

For projects which are considered feasible, the study defines the technical framework and the scope of the proposed system. The scope is defined in terms of:-

•   The functions of the existing system which are to be investigated during systems analysis.

- The functions which are likely to require change and where change has been assessed as feasible.

- The level of benefit to be achieved.

The technical framework consists of an outline design for the system. The use of facilities such as database and real time software should be identified and the necessary degree of complexity established eg the extent to which the data is held under DBMS control and whether it is updated in real time. At various stages during the project, these guidelines will need to be reviewed in the light of more detailed study.

The structured systems analysis method, some other analysis techniques, sizing and cost/ benefit analysis, are all applied at the level appropriate for a feasibility study, but it must be remembered that the objectives is only to assess feasibility; the majority of the detailed work comes later.

2.3.3   Perform Systems Analysis

The systems analysis phase of a project is concerned with producing a detailed specification of the new system in business terms. The specification serves as the basis for user agreement on the facilities to be provided and the performance targets to be met. It contains all the information necessary for system design. The primary requirements are to build fruitful communications with users and to produce a thorough understanding and definition of the systems.

Structured systems analysis is used in MODUS. It is concerned with:-

- Functional analysis, where the requirement is to build a progressively more detailed picture of the functions of an existing or new system. Activity diagrams are used as an aid to the investigation of an existing system or to the creative process of defining the new system.

- Data analysis, where the requirement is to gain a thorough and unambiguous understanding and definition of the data and their interdependences.

- Analysis of requirements, where the requirements of the application area are identified and then matched against the existing system in order to assess the need for change.

Each of these aspects of analysis requires techniques and a procedural framework within which they can be applied. The techniques help the analyst to cope with the complexity of systems and to ensure that the systems eventually proposed do meet genuine requirements which serve the objectives of the organisation, and are unambiguously and completely specified. The procedure must also provide a basis for estimating the work required and progressing the work during the phase. Clear review points at which walkthroughs can be held are also necessary. Documentation standards are very important for the effective communication between the analyst and users, designers and other team members.

2.3.4 Design System

The system design phase of a project is concerned with transforming the logical view of a system into a physical specification of programs, files, inputs, outputs and controls. The primary objective during system design is to produce a system which is readily maintainable while taking explicit account of performance targets and machine characteristics.

The method leads initially to a logical model of the required computer system and then to a first-pass physical design. The first-pass design represents the simplest, most maintainable view of the system. This design is then progressively refined to the extent necessary to meet the system performance targets., Program specifications are produced as a by-product of the method itself rather than as a separate task following design. The approach is appropriate for real time and database systems, as well as for conventional batch systems.

Techniques help the designer by providing criteria by which the quality of design can be assessed, hence aiding the identification of programs and files. The designer needs to rely less on intuition and experience.

Procedures are necessary to ensure that design is carried out thoroughly and as with each phase, to provide a basis for estimating and progressing. Periodic reviews ensure that programmers and operations staff become progressively more involved.

The documentation consists of a definition of the structure of the design and general aspects, such as security and resource requirements. Detailed definition of the design is also part of the method in the form of program specification, detailed file or database definitions and detailed inputs, outputs, terminal layouts and conversational sequences.

2.3.5 Develop Programs

The programming phase of a project is concerned with the production of individually tested programs from the specifications produced during system design. The primary objective is to produce reliable programs which are easily maintainable. The structured programming techniques are used to provide a method for producing well-designed programs. The method uses the established technique of file structure analysis as the means of producing a logical design for the program. A driving file is selected and its structure is matched with the structure of the other files used by the program. The structure of the driving file is enhanced to reflect correspondences and processing requirements. The enhanced structure becomes the basis for the design of the program defined in terms of a logical module hierarchy chart and design language. The design is then translated into the appropriate programming language by applying well-defined coding conventions.

2.3.6   Test System

Structured testing is used and is concerned with demonstrating that the developed system operates as intended. There are two stages of testing. These are program and system testing. The planning of testing starts in systems analysis. These plans are further refined during system design and programming. Program testing must demonstrate the reliability of individual programs. It is planned for each program and is concerned with testing each logical module.

The purpose of system testing is to demonstrate the reliability of the system as a whole. It is concerned with the accuracy of processing, the consistency of interfaces within the system and between systems and in demonstrating that security and recovery procedures work. The overall system is also shown to run within the expected physical resources.

2.3.7   Size System

In parallel with the development in phases of a system, it is sized to determine its use of machine resources. The technique used is technical design control. Using this technique, the utilizations of important computer resources, such as CPU and disk channel time, is predicted. This prediction is first carried out in the feasibility study, updated following analysis, done in detail in design, and refined through the various testing phases. Thus an up to date prediction of the resource requirements under peak load conditions is maintained. With critically timed or potentially expensive systems, a valuable guide to where modification is necessary is thus obtained.

2.3.8   Perform Acceptance Testing

Acceptance testing is concerned with ensuring that the system meets the requirements of the user and is acceptable to the operations department. Planning commences following system analysis. Acceptance testing is organised so that the system is used in a manner as close as possible to the live environment. It should be used as an opportunity to train user staff and can be extended to include parallel running. The MODUS testing method covers acceptance testing as part of overall testing. It is integrated with program and systems testing in such a way as to enable the differing objectives to be satisfied while limiting unnecessary repetition of planning, creating data for, and carrying out, tests.

2.3.9   Implement System

The planning of implementation commences during the feasibility study phase. At that stage, it is necessary to produce an outline plan and for some events, such as machine installation or file conversation, it may then be necessary to plan in detail. The implementation plan is progressively refined during the project as more detailed information becomes available. Planning must include:-

- Scheduling of implementation.

- Data conversion.

- Acquisition and training of staff.

- Clerical system design.

- Production of operating manuals.

- Conversion to new system.

The design of clerical procedures to support the use of the computer system is carried out in parallel with system design for the automated part of the system. These clerical procedures must specify how all manual activities within the scope of the systems development are to be carried out. During the systems analysis phase, these activities will have been identified in logical terms and physical interfaces to the automated part specified. During clerical system design, O & M techniques may be applied to define the most effective way of carrying out the clerical activities.

2.3.10 Review System Post Implementation

There are two major aspects to the review of a system development project:-

- Review of the development process.

- Review of the effectiveness of the system.

In practice, it will usually be appropriate to review the development process as soon as implementation is complete. A review of the effectiveness of the system cannot be carried out until there has been time for the benefits to become apparent. A review of the development process will include performance against budget and schedule and adherence to standards and their effectiveness. A view on the quality of design must also be formed. The results of this review should be used to improve the team members or their successors. A review of the effectiveness of the system must include an assessment of user satisfaction and a re-evaluation of the cost/benefit balance. To enable refinement of the physical aspects of the system, a measure of how well the system met performance targets and how easy it is to operate and maintain must be obtained. The results of this review should be used to improve the quality of standards and training so that future systems may be more effective.

2.3.11 Walkthroughs

In the development method described, there are many checkpoints at the project phase end and on completion of the more detailed activities within phases. The involvement of project staff other than those who carried out the work is desirable. The method of conducting the reviews - walkthroughs. By using appropriate techniques, a constructive atmosphere within the walkthrough can be achieved, which is effective in trapping errors at a moderate cost in time spent.

2.4   C.A.C.I. INC

CACI were founded in 1962. They position themselves as a leader in such diverse areas as information systems, engineering, logistics, proprietary software products, and information products and services in market analysis. The European headquarters are based in Richmond, UK. This operation started in 1975 and specialises in structured systems development methods and disciplines and market analysis. Their main focus is on the application of the former methods to all phases of the system life cycle from strategy studies through to system implementation. CACI also promote training, which is based on their structured method.

CACI is recognised as one of Europe's leading consultancies in database and TP systems. Much of its activities involve data analysis, database design, communications network design, systems implementation and systems conversion. D2S2 is a systems development methodology, most or all of which has been applied on the majority of CACI projects in Europe since 1975. It differs from alternative methodologies in the emphasis placed on data sharing; in treating the analysis of data and its inherent structure independently from the various applications which may use this data, as opposed to the functionally oriented approaches which inevitably lead to systems and files biased towards specific business problems, with no guarantee of flexibility or potential integration.

Until 1977, CACI had neglected the "functional analysis" half of their methodology, but more complex projects led them to the realisation that "entity modelling" could not replace an equally detailed analysis of the business functions. Gradually techniques such as "functional decomposition" and "data flow diagrams" were introduced on CACI projects. Another project led to the development of "entity life cycles". D2S2 has continued to evolve, so as to be applicable to all stages of the systems life cycle and to all types of data handling systems, rather than merely those using a DBMS.

There are two main activities within the methodology (4):-

- Functional analysis is used to define the functions which make business operate, for example handling orders, maintaining plant, controlling borrowing, paying staff.

- Entity analysis is concerned with finding out what the business needs in order to operate, expressed in terms of the types of things it needs and the relevant facts about these things: For example, it may need people, plants, orders and accounts and it may need to know the date of birth, sex and name of each person.

These two activities, functional analysis and entity analysis, are normally completed in parallel as complementary operations, each providing the other with better insight into the business. Since details of both the data and its processing are essential to the design of an effective database, both activities are always used in preparation for database design.

Where the methodology is being used for other purposes, however, only one of the two may be necessary. The conversion of a system, for instance, depends very much on the structure of the data. When converting from one data structure to another - for example, from conventional files to database - both the source data structure and the target data structure can usefully be compared using the results of entity analysis alone.

In figure 2.5 the phases in data analysis are shown as part of the tasks involved in the design of a system.

ENTITY ANALYSIS	FUNCTIONAL ANALYSIS	ANALYSIS
DATABASE DESIGN	APPLICATION DESIGN	Applied Related Tasks DESIGN
DATABASE CREATION	PROGRAM DEVELOPMENT	IMPLEMENTATION

Figure 2.5 - Data Analysis as Part of System Design

Although its main use is in implementing large and complex database systems, data analysis is a pragmatic approach developed to meet practical needs. Other major uses to which it has been put in the last five years are:-

• Evaluation of the suitability of application packages. The entities and functions inherent in the business are compared with those supported by the package.

• Evaluation of the structuring capability of competing database management systems: The rival DBMSs are compared using the structure of the actual business data as a benchmark with which to test the ease of mapping the business to the DBMS.

- System conversion : The comparison of the data structure for conversion with the target data structure, indicates the simplest possible conversion process.

- Data dictionary : Data analysis is an essential pre-requisite for populating a data dictionary which is to be used for the development and maintenance of future applications.

- Distributed processing : The investigation of the existing distribution of the entities and business functions indicates where distribution of data and processing could take place.

- Application development strategies : The strategy is based on the evaluation of the business functions, to determine where computerization would be most beneficial and the clustering of those functions into logical applications for implementation.

- Policy studies : Feasibility studies into the need for and viability of a database (or shared data environment) and transaction processing systems.

- Data control systems, security and audit procedures : The nature of the existing data is examined and all the interactions and redundencies documented. This process provides the basis for control and for security and audit procedures.

- Organisation studies : The study of a business' functions, related to who has to carry out the functions and how, indicates where the introduction of standard practices would help the enterprise: For example, where there is duplication of effort or inefficient allocation of tasks, and where new jobs might be needed or the responsibilities for existing jobs need to be reviewed.

2.5. LEARMONTH & BURCHETT MANAGEMENT SYSTEMS (LBMS)

LBMS was formed in 1977 by Roger Learmonth and Rainer Burchett, when they broke from BIS. They have offices in London, Bristol, Houston and Sacramento. They have grown from a staff of 20 in 1980 to just over 130 at the end of 1986. Their annual turnover has grown from £3 million in 1983/84 to £4.7 million in 1985/86. This change in the fortunes of the group is tied to the adoption of their methodology by the UK government. LBMS provide the following services to their customers:

- Consultancy - Assignments cover all aspects of information technology from strategic planning through to system implementation.

- Methodology -   The LBMS approach to the varying aspects of DP systems development projects is incorporated in a series of methods as shown in figure 2.6

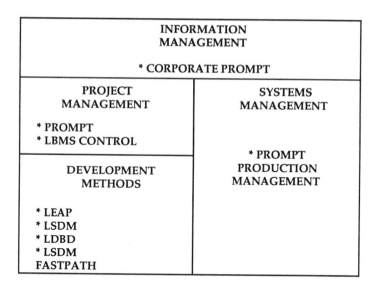

INFORMATION MANAGEMENT * CORPORATE PROMPT	
PROJECT MANAGEMENT * PROMPT * LBMS CONTROL	SYSTEMS MANAGEMENT
DEVELOPMENT METHODS * LEAP * LSDM * LDBD * LSDM FASTPATH	* PROMPT PRODUCTION MANAGEMENT

Figure 2.6: LBMS Methodology Components

The various stages shown in figure 2.6 are as follows:

- CORPORATE PROMPT : provides guidelines for the organisation and procedures needed at a strategic level to manage information as a corporate resource.

- PROMPT project management : provides guidelines on roles and responsibilities, quality assurance, planning and progress reporting needed for development projects.

- LBMS CONTROL : provides guidelines and techniques for effective management and control of a LSDM development project.

- LEAP ; is a business system planning method for the creation of strategic information technology plans.

- LSDM : the commercial version of SSADM. It provides structured, procedural and documentation standards for the analysis and design phases of systems projects.

- LDBD ; is a subset of LSDM covering data analysis and database design. LDBD incorporate design rules, timing criteria and running tips for all major DBMS. It was the first LBMD method.

- LSDM FASTPATH : is reduced version of LSDM for smaller projects with tight time-scales.

- PROMPT production control : sets our management and technical activities required from the running of established information systems within an organisation.

- Design Automation Tools - KBMS methods are to be automated and they have targeted the IBM PC as the environment. In which they will operate. There are currently 3 products they provide:-

  - SUPER-MATE: this provides a graphic front-end and data gathering tool for LEAP, which supports the LEAP interview process, by identifying effective current.future systems and creating strategic data models/target states

  - AUTO-MATE: this provides a design and documentation aid for LSDM and SSADM users. It supports data flow diagrams, logic data structure diagrams, and entity life history diagrams. In addition reports and panels can be prototyped.

  - DATA-MATE: this automates data analysis and can be used in conjunction with AUTO-MATE or independently. It provides a diagram editor for entity modelling and entity, relationship and attribute documentation. There is a choice of guidance through normalisation process by use of an expert system.

  LBMS is participating in a consortium, partially funded by the Alvey Directorate to produce a comprehensive Integrated Project Support Environment (IPSE).

- Training - LBMS offer courses not only in their methods and the use of their tools but also in structured methods, basis systems analysis and design, data analysis, database development and relational databases. Residential courses are normally presented at a hotel on the south coast of the UK. Non-residential courses are normally presented in London.

LBMS Structured Development method (LSDM) has grown on the firm base of another LBMS product - LBMS Database Design, LDBD. LSDM is the result of a joint project with the CCTA.

2.5..1 Underlying Principles of LSDM

LSDM has been constructed on a number of principles which together make it an effective way of developing systems and with significant advantages over "traditional" methods of systems analysis and design. They are:-

- System structures should be determined by data structures. It is a data driven method and not a function driven one.

- Logical and physical concepts are separated. A detailed logical design is developed before hardware, software and implementation constraints are taken into account.

- Development should be iterative, in that an eventual cost-effective solution is arrived at via the development of partially correct views, based the parallel development of three crucial system views - data flows, data structures and time cycles. Reliance is not placed in one single "pet" technique. Validation and consistency checking between the different definitions lead to an objectively accurate total system model.

- The conversion of logical to physical design is covered in a prescriptive way. Rules and guidelines are provided for the definition of files/databases, and programs and runflows.

- Detailed performance, estimation and optimization should be carried out on the physical design before committing to implementation.

- The user should be actively involved throughout all levels of the development process. By contributing to the achievement of a system which meets his needs he will become committed to its success.

- A top-down approach is taken, a start is made at a high level, initially showing the broad picture and then allowing gradual and controlled decomposition into increased levels of detail.

- Regular and formalised reviews are incorporated which ensure that all work done is critically received for quality, completeness and applicability.

2.5.2 LSDM in the Project Life Cycle

LSDM addresses the pre-programming phases of system development. The two major phases involved are System Analysis, defining what has to be done and System Design, defining how it will be done. Many projects have a preliminary, feasibility, phase for which LSDM can also be used. Figure 2.7 shows the different phases of LSDM (5).

2.5.3 Input to LSDM

Every organisation is likely to have its own view and of where computer systems development fits into its structure and operations. LSDM, as a generally applicable development method must be able to cope with widely differing project circumstances. There is, therefore, no detailed specification for the "Statement of Requirement" which is the input to LSDM. It can be as simple as a few lines broadly outlining the area for investigation, or as detailed as a preliminary study which may have involved some man

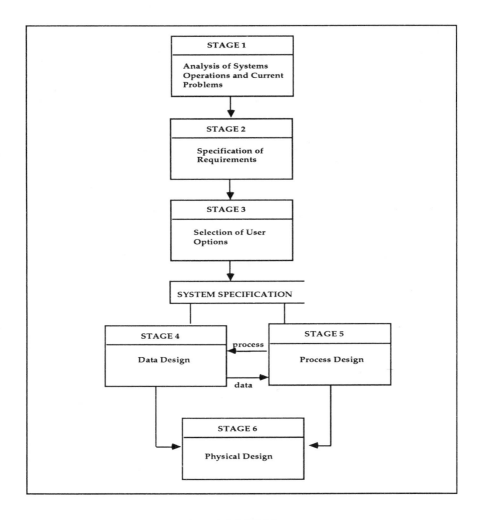

Figure 2.7 LSDM Stages

years of effort to produce. Obviously the more detailed the Statement of Requirement, the less effort is required in the Analysis Phase.

2.5.4 Output from LSDM

If the input is necessarily ill-defined, the output is not. LSDM produces the following detailed documentation :-

- Program specifications and file specifications or database schema's for the target hardware/software environment;

- User and operations procedure specifications;

- Plans for the post-design phases of project development.

The programming phase can begin immediately after the completion of the final LSDM stage.

2.5.5 Analysis Phase

The objective of the Analysis study is to create a detailed specification of the User Requirements, ie what the system has to do and to agree with the Users what levels of service and performance are required. The stages in this phase are:-

- Analysis of Current Operations and Problems.

- Specification of Requirements, in terms of what the system must provide rather than how it will work.

- Selection of user options, in which the user selects a system for implementation from a menu of possibilities, each having differing service levels, costs/benefits and development implications.

2.5.6 Design Phase

The objective of System design is to define the structure and content of the system; how it is to provide the required services and how it is to be implemented. The stages are:-

- Data Design, in which the detailed logical structure and the content of each component is defined;

- Process Design, in which individual processes are specified in detail;

- Physical Design, which involves the conversion of the logical design to one for implementation on a particular hardware/software environment, refined to meet performance requirements to within fine tuning limits, and specified in detail, together with the plans for the remaining phases of system development.

2.5.7 Feasibility Study

The objective of any Feasibility Study is to justify further development by examining business and technical feasibility and the potential costs and benefits, as far as they can be ascertained at this early stage, of the potential system. It defines the scope, terms of reference and structure of the succeeding (Analysis) phase. It can be done by applying the Analysis stages of LSDM, but at a higher level than envisaged for normal analysis and not necessarily using all the techniques. The level to which the stages are applied will vary with circumstance. Whether a Feasibility Study is carried out will depend on project size and timescale, and on how much preliminary work is carried out before beginning the development process. Where LSDM is used in a Feasibility Study prior to using it for a normal Analysis phase the term "two-pass analysis" is used.

2.5.8 LSDM Techniques

LSDM uses a number of techniques. Together with the detailed rules and guidelines for their use they form the procedural standard element of the Method. They are, individually, not unique and have been well proven in many project circumstances. The major techniques used in the LBMS development method are:-

- Logical Data Structuring Technique (LDST) - a method for deriving entity/data models.

- Data Flow Diagrams (DFDs) - a method of representing flows of information through a system and between the system and the outside world.

- Entity Life Histories (ELHs) - a technique for developing a model of how the system cycles operate and how events must be handled by the system.

- Process Outlines - a method of converting ELHs into definitions describing how transactions must be processed by the system.

- . Third Normal Form (TNF) data analysis - a technique for defining data and creating unambiguous logical data sets.

- First Cut Data Design - rules for converting logical data models into physical files/databases.

- First Cut Programs - rules for converting logical data flows into transactions and program run flows.

- Physical Design Control (PDC) - a process for tuning designs to meet acceptable performance criteria.

In addition to the above, LSDM also requires the use of other techniques which can be regarded as falling within the province of a Project Management system, management and control standards. These techniques include:-

- Quality Assurance reviews to ensure the accuracy and completeness and to indicate project progress.

- Formal documentation, in the form of reports, produced at significant project milestones. These formal documents incorporate LSDM deliverables documented in accordance with SSADM documentation standards.

- A method of controlling the progress of project development which provides a standard approach to the detailed evaluation, planning, implementation, and progress monitoring of project phases.

These areas are addressed by LBMS CONTROL and/or PROMPT.

The use of the LSDM techniques is covered by a detailed set of explanatory rules and guidelines. These allow development staff to initially use a "cook book" approach through each of the stages.

2.5.9 Three Views of the System

There is a strong tendency for development methods to offer a main technique and then build the entire development task list around this technique. LSDM does not fall into this trap. There are three views of a system that LSDM provides:-

- The data structure is firstly identified, mapped and validated. LDST entity modelling, TNF data analysis and CLD techniques are used to accomplish this.

- Secondly, Data Flow Diagramming is used to decompose the functions to provide the second view; namely the information flow through the system.

- Finally, the third view of a system is how it behaves over time. This accomplished is LSDM using ELH's and Process Outlines.

2.6.   JAMES MARTIN ASSOCIATES (JMA)

JMA started life in 1981 as the European arm of DMW. The latter was formed in the USA in 1971 to provide professional service for the solution of management problems and to specialise in the provision of service in the areas of telecommunications, database and information systems. The European group was formed to offer the full range of DMW's services in Europe. The group was reformed in 1982/83 under the title of James Martin Associates with headquarters in Wimbledon, UK.

JMA offers a wide range of consulting services from top-level management studies to the provision of individual front line consultants for system tuning and application development. The consultancy support takes the form of regular "surgery" visits where progress in the use of the methods is reviewed and problem areas discussed and resolved.

The main task for JMA when it was formed in 1981 was the formulation of Information Engineering. This was done under the leadership of Ian Palmer, who was their first Technical Director, by combining the CACI data and functional analysis methodology with the ideas of James Martin into a commercial marketable product.

Information engineering encompasses a set of inter-related disciplines, supported by methodologies which are used to develop data structures and systems that satisfy an organisations mission and functional objectives. These systems are based on data and data relationships which are independent of data flow, but depend on business policy and are user driven ie Systems development and data processes change. Once stable data structures are established, procedures can be developed based on data change brought about by a combination of events and conditions. These data changes include additions, deletions, modifications and retrievals. Figure 2.8 is a model which graphically illustrates the different methodologies used in Information Engineering and how they relate to one another.

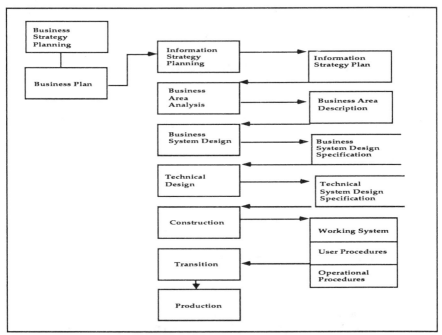

Figure 2.8 : Stages of an Information Engineering Development Cycle

The full set of stages (6) recognised by Information Engineering in a systems development cycle is shown in Figure 2.8 are :-

- Business Strategy Planning concerns the development of an overall business plan with goals and objectives for the enterprise.

- Information Strategy Planning develops, from the business objectives, an initial information architecture for the enterprise, identifies areas where automated support is appropriate and prepares a plan to show how these areas should be dealt with.

- Business Area Analysis takes areas identified in the plan, analyses their components in complete detail, determines all of the associations and interactions between them and develops detailed models which can be cross-checked and validated: From these, a selection is made of the parts users wish to have supported in their systems.

- Business Systems Design takes the processes which are to be supported and works out with the user the best way to handle them as a practical set of tasks and dialogues.

- Technical Design fits the user requirements to the technology available: It provides the full input and output formats, the design of the physical database structure and the design of programs and transactions.

- Construction is the coding of programs and database descriptions, the assembling and testing of the complete system and the preparation of all operations and user procedures.

- Transition deals with the parallel-running, cut-over and fan-out period of the completed system and with any conversion or bridging that may be needed.

- Production covers the working life of the system, the monitoring of its performance and its tuning and maintenance.

These stages are the major elements of the task structure in the methodology. They may be varied significantly, depending on the tools and techniques available. Each stage contains specific tasks and techniques needed to produce the deliverable products required to satisfy the fundamental processes which the stage encompasses.

2.6.1 Business Strategy Planning

Experience has established the importance of corporate objectives as the basis for formulating strategic plans. The existence of the enterprise is assumed with its present products, services, markets and channels. This is used as a starting point. From it, objectives are established for the future and strategies are developed to enable the objectives to be met. The end product of business strategy planning will be a business plan, indicating overall business goals and strategies. This shows the main business functions, the organisational structure and the objectives established for each function.

2.6.2 Information Strategy Planning

Information Strategy planning results in an information systems development strategy describing business requirements and priorities. These form the underlying rationale for information systems needs and from them, aspects of three architectures are derived:-

- The information architecture of the business, expressed as data subject areas, business functions and their interactions.

- An application systems architecture proposed to support the information needs.

- A statement of direction for the technical architecture composed of computer hardware, software and communications. The strategy includes a broad cost benefit and specific migration plans and shows how, from all of this information, a plan for systems development has been prepared, including work programmes for high-priority projects.

2.6.3 Business Area Analysis

For an identified business area within the scope of the information systems development strategy, a detailed study is carried out of its data, its business functions and the information required to fulfill those functions. This leads to identification of entity types and of the specific business processes and their information inputs and outputs. These are analysed in detail and their names, interactions, meanings, quantities, rules and business algorithms documented. An important feature is that maximum involvement of end users in the specification of requirements, priorities and facilities is recommended. From this information, a detailed statement of the business requirement for information systems in the business area is produced. Prototyping techniques, using Fourth Generation languages, may be used in some cases to clarify or verify details of the requirement.

At the end of business area analysis a business area description is prepared, showing business functions and processes performed in the area with their usage patterns in the business processes. The properties of all these objects are documented. From these details it is possible to identify the broad nature of likely computer support required for business processes; to define the scope of one or more design areas for which business systems can be designed; to prepare a work program and resource estimates for the design areas.

2.6.4 Business System Design

For the whole or a major part of a business area analysed, the facts gathered during analysis are used to design a system to meet the identified business requirements. The design includes all those parts of the system directly relevant to its users including transactions, dialogues and controls. It is kept as independent as possible of the technology to be employed in implementation. Prototyping techniques, using Fourth Generation languages, may be used to replace many of the tasks traditionally gone through in this stage. An important objectives of this stage is that it should complete the system deign to the extent possible without pre-judging technical issues. It is also heavily user oriented and requires agreement of the users on the ways in which they will interact with the system.

The final product from business system design is a business system specification showing, for each business process, the consolidated documentation of information flows and user procedures and for each computer process, a consolidated and confirmed version of the results of business area analysis, plus the dialogue design, screens, reports and other user interfaces and adjustments to the data usage patterns. From this, a detailed scoping of the intended computer systems is prepared together with a work programme and resource estimates for the next stage. A key technique in this stage involves representing the logic and data usage of procedures in the form of structured action diagrams. These can be translated directly into Fourth Generation language statements.

2.6.5 Technical Design

For the computerised aspects of the business systems specified, the facts gathered during analysis are used to design those, coding the system which are dependent upon the computer technical environment. This is carried out in sufficient detail for construction and operation to be adequately costed. This design includes physical data structures, computer programs, operational procedures and interfaces. The level of detail in the design is dependent upon the selection of implementation vehicle, eg system generators have much of the technical architecture predefined.

The end result of technical design is therefore a technical specification containing database designs and procedure designs in the form of database-oriented action diagrams and the application system technical design. These include batch runs, finalised conversation flows and definition of programming work units. The specification also includes the technical architecture and standards for the system, the hardware and software environment selected, its mode of use and specific standards and conventions proposed. Finally it identifies the content of the construction and transition stages and gives a work programme and resource estimates for these stages.

2.6.6 Construction

For each phase identified during design, a system is put together. This includes installation of equipment, establishing files, setting up procedures and specifying, coding and testing programs. The aim in the construction stage is to develop an application system, as defined in the technical specification, which meets the targets of timescale and budge, is of an acceptable quality and which contains all necessary operating and user procedures. The stage can be regarded as complete once the defined acceptance criteria for the application are met satisfactorily.

2.6.7 Transition

Transition is the phased replacement of existing procedures and files with the new system and data structures. It is governed by the transition plan, including a work programme and resource estimates, which is normally finalised in parallel with the construction phase, although it is not really dependent on the outcome. Transition can be regarded as successful when the system operates for a specified period within defined tolerances as regards performance, error date and usability and passes its post-implementation review.

2.6.8 Production

Production is the successful operation of the system, with tuning and modification as necessary, until eventually the transition stage in some other project replaces the systems built in this project. The main objectives during production are to maintain service levels and functional performance during the lifetime of the system and to respond promptly and effectively to changes in business requirements.

2.7   THE NEXT GENERATION

The advent of fourth generation languages has shown that the current batch of methodologies are not flexible enough to take on new techniques easily. It is difficult for them to take on new techniques such as prototyping and new tools such as application generators. In Great Britain, this has led to a new breed of methodology vendors to arise. These vendors are in the main consultants, who have worked with fourth generation products and relational databases very closely. Examples are Southcourt, Systems Advisers and Softwright.

2.7.1 Southcourt

Southcourt have developed a methodology called Evolutionary Systems Management (ESM). Figure 2.9 shows the stages of the method.

There are three implementation approaches to ESM :-

- Business based Information Technology Strategy (BBITS) : this is for the executive for strategic top down work;

- Evolutionary Systems Planning (ESP) : this is used by DP managers for the tactical planning of systems;

- Evolutionary Systems Implementation (ESI) : this use structured prototyping to develop and implement the required systems.

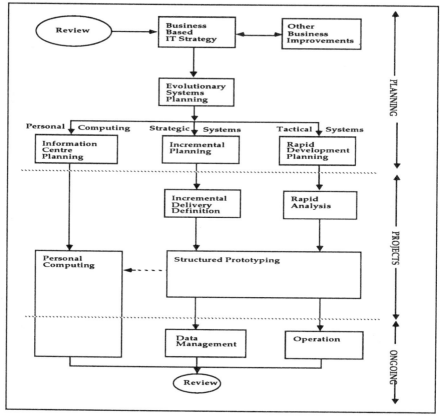

Figure 2.9 : Evolutionary Systems Management

The concept of prototyping and structured design have been molded together , as well as the integration of strategic and tactical planning of information systems requirements.

2.7.2 Systems Advisers

Systems Advisers Ltd was formed in 1981 by a group of management consultants. It provides high-level consulting in data processing and information technology. SA special-ises in the management of the corporate information resource. They advise clients on the profitable application of computers and information technology. An important aspect of their work is in the training of both technical and non-technical staff, through public seminars and in-house training programmes. In 1983, Systems Advisers do Brazil Ltda. was formed to service a growing clientele in South America.

SA's methodology is entitled "Information Resource Management". It is built upon JMA's

Information Engineering methodology with certain additional features; prominent among which are project management, and the style of the information resource planning stage. Figure 2.10 shows the stages of the methodology.

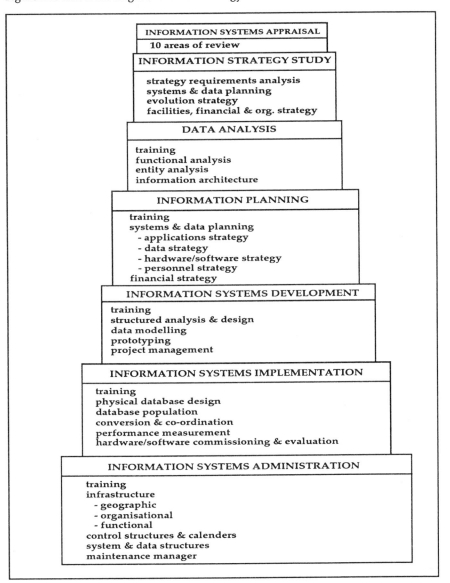

Figure 2.10 : Information Resource Management

The methodology has been designed to encourage user participation in the management of the Information Resource and the philosophy behind the use of each technique has been to simplify as far as possible, so that the technique can be applied by the user himself without extensive training, or use of computerised tools. They offer the methodology in the form of a consultancy and training package. In 1987 (7), they developed a prototyping approach to information systems planning.

2.7.3   The Response to the Fourth Generation

The CCTA during 1987 commissioned work to be done to develop an interface between SSADM and ICL's QuickBuild product set (8). A manual and a training course were developed, and trials were undertaken of its usage. Prototyping played a major part in this adjunct to the basic methodology. Version 4 of SSADM is now being developed, and I believe that this version of the method will contain many of the prototyping ideas developed for the QuickBuild Interface, plus additional work to better support relational databases and distribution.

James Martin Associates answer to the Fourth Generation is a switch away from advocating fourth generation tools as the answer to DP managers problems, and advocating of the adoption of their CASE (computer Aided Software Engineering) tool. This was developed with Texas Instruments and is called the Information Engineering Facility. The CASE tool started out as a sophisticated 'front-end' CASE tool; one which supported all the diagramming techniques for Information Engineering, an analyst's tool. It now supports the generation of COBOL with embedded SQL programs. The methodology has remained static over the last three years.

2.8   WHERE TO NEXT ?

Current methodologies are still not complete. In my view, there are two major areas that are still outstanding :-

*   Testing;

*   Maintenance.

Although testing has always been part of most methodologies, its techniques have not evolved at the same pace as those for analysis, design and coding. Many people have argued that testing becomes less important, as more of the system life cycle is automated. If anything it becomes more important, because testing is being brought higher and higher up the life cycle.

All methodologies that I have seen pay lip service to maintenance, but none of them really tackle the problem that faces all DP departments, that of "How do we maintain all of our existing systems?". A new term has appeared in the literature in 1988, that of "Reverse

Engineering". The idea of reverse Engineering is that by means of a tool that reads your old programs, documentation about your existing systems can be produced, so that you can use your development methodology to carry out any changes. But at the moment, there are few tools available to allow you to do this.

Reference

1. TOO MANY METHODOLOGIES, R.M.Tagg, Data Analysis Update, edited by G.J.Baker, British Comouter Society Database Specialist Group, April 1983.

2. STRUCTURED SYSTEMS DEVELOPMENT TECHNIQUES : STRATEGIC PLAN-NING TO SYSTEMS TESTING, G.Collins and G.Blay, Pitman Bokks Ltd, 1982.

3. STRUCTURED TECHNIQUES OVERVIEW, Professional Services Abstract no. 29-211, BIS Applied Systems.

4. DATA ANALYSIS, Rosemary Rock-Evans, IPC Electrical-Elctronic Press Ltd, 1981.

5. INTRODUCTION TO LSDM, LBMS Brochure 1987.

6. INFORMATION ENGINEERING - A METHODOLOGY TO MATCH FOURTH GENERATION TOOLs, I.G.Macdonald, James Martin Assoicates, 1984.

7. INFORMATION SYSTEMS PLANNING - A PROTOTYPING APPROACH, R.J.A.Jarvis, edited by P.Feldman, L.Bhabuta and S.Holloway, Information Management and Planning, DATABASE 87, British Computer Society Database Specialist Group, 1987 (to be published by Gower Technical Press).

8. ICL QUICKBUILD SSADM IMPLEMENTATION GUIDE, Information Systems Engineering Report, Draft for Development, CCTA, Jan. 1987.

FURTHER READING

*   Information Systems Design methodologies : A Comparative Review, T.W.Olle, H.G.Sol and A.A.Verrjin-Stuart, North Holland, 1982.

*   A Taxonomy of current approaches to Systems Analysis, A.T.Wood-Harper and G.Fitzgerald, The Computer Journal, 25, No 1, 1985.

*   Information Systems Design Methodologies : a feature analysis, T.W.Olle, H.G.Sol and C.J.Tully, North Holland, 1983.

*   Ending the Computer Conspiracy : the thinking person's guide to successful systems, C.Conder, McGraw Hill, 1985.

- Application System Development methodologies - solution or problem ?, D.Connor, Savant Instsiute, 1982.

- Feature Analysis of contemporary Information Systems Methodologies : a collective view, R.N.Maddison, G.J.Baker, G.Fitzgerald, K.Humble, J.H.T.Sory, N.Stokes and J.R.G.Wood, Open University, 1982.

- Information Engineering, volumes I and II, J.Martin, Savant Institute, 1981.

- Information Systems Development : a data base approach, D.E.Avison, Blackwell Scientific Publication, 1985.

3. INFORMATION RESOURCE PLANNING

3.1. INTRODUCTION

The prime objective of information resource planning is to produce, develop and maintain tactical (short term) and strategic (long term) plans for the development and implementation of information systems and the provision of the necessary hardware, software and organisation resources to support the plan.

The secondary objectives are to define information systems objectives in terms of benefits to the organisation, match these objectives to the overall business objectives and goals, and create a favourable environment for tactical project initiation and control.

The main tool used in information resource planning in the Information Systems Architecture which consists of 4 parts :-

*   A Business Architecture, which represents the organisation's business requirements.

*   A Data Architecture, which represents the data and processes that match the organisation's business requirements.

*   An Application Architecture, which represents the information systems that are required to support the organisation's business requirements.

*   A Technical Architecture, which represents the technology required to support that data and the information systems requirements.

Information resource planning uses a combination of strategic planning methods to collect, analyse and document information obtained.

This information is then used to create an Information systems Architecture which will in turn be used to provide a series of plans, both tactical and strategic. Figure 3.1 shows the various stages in Information Resource Planning Module.

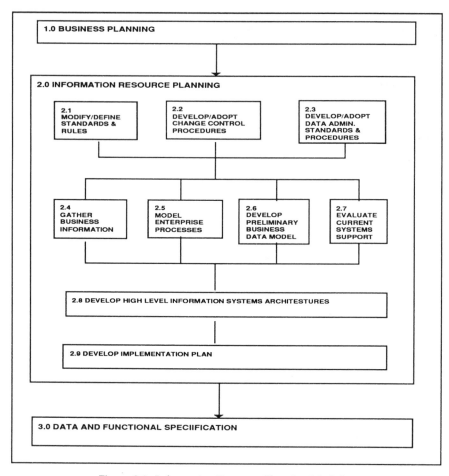

Figure 3.1 : Information Resource Planning Modules

3.2. STANDARDS, PROCEDURES AND GUIDELINES

Before commencing on the in-depth study of the organisation, it is necessary to look at what standards, procedures and guidelines an organisation has in place. The first three phases of Information Resource Planning do just this.

Firstly the existing Methodology standards and rules are collected and analysed, and where necessary modified and defined.

It is recognised that the Information Resource Planning study will be an iterative process and that many changes will occur: It is therefore important that change control procedures are in place. If an organisation has these procedures in place, they will be evaluated and where necessary modifications may be recommended. In the case of organisations with no procedures, a standard set of procedures will be derived.

It is important to recognise that Data Administration is the function within an organisation, which has as its objective ensuring the provision of corporate data resource to satisfy, in a cost effective manner, the information requirements of that organisation. To ensure the smooth operation of the Data Administration function, policies, standards, guidelines and procedures pertinent to the Information Resource Planning study need to be defined. The main ones to be concerned with are as follows :-

- Data Naming;

- Security, Privacy and Integrity;

- Government Regulations, such as the Data Protection legislation;

- Data Dictionary usage;

- Data Entity diagrams;

- Subject data groups;

- Data Analysis techniques.

3.3. GATHER BUSINESS INFORMATION

Before it is possible to carry out the detailed Information Resource Planning study, it is necessary to carry out an overview of the organisation. The Information Resource Planning study team will need to gain a general appreciation of the business. This background information will include:-

- an examination of the goals of the organisation;

- the critical success factors as perceived by the executive;

- the mission of the organisation;

- the purpose of the organisation;

- the company structure;

- the roles of the key personnel.

This information will enable the information resource planning study team to construct an interview plan.

3.3.1. Goals of the Organisation

It used to be said that organisations had just the one goal of profit maximization. The truth is that businesses have a number of goals. These could include any of the following:-

- Increasing the size of the organisation;

- Long term survival;

- The welfare of their employees;

- Improving their public image.

It could be that there are major long term goals which businesses fulfill, such as maximizing the return on capital, whilst having shorter term aims, such as increasing turnover.

3.3.2. Critical Success Factors

In most industries there are usually three to six factors that determine success: These key jobs must be done exceedingly well for an organisation to be successful. The CSF approach asks top management in the organisation to identify these factors. In a business, the critical success factors relate to those aspects of the business that will ensure competitive performance.

3.3.3. The Mission and Purpose of the Organisation

The mission and purpose statement are often quite different from the critical success factors. They represent long-range vision or an end-point which the organisation wishes to achieve.

3.3.4. Company Structure and the Roles of Key Personnel

It is important for the information resource planning study team to consider the structure of the organisation and the roles played by members of the management team. Without this knowledge, it is not possible to decide on the people to interview, and the level and subject matter of the questions to ask.

3.4.   MODEL BUSINESS PROCESSES

Taking the Organisation Structure chart for the previous phase, the information resource planning study team determine the various functions of the organisation; discovering the answers to the questions

"What resources, services and products are managed ?"

And

"What is done ?"

Business Processes are collections of business actions, which must be completed in order to accomplish the goals and objectives of the organisation or its sub-group. Each high-level business process is directly related to a business functional area or resource. Accurately defining these processes is very important,. As they form the basis for the information systems architecture and key data requirements. The basic steps involved in defining business processes is represented in Figure 3.2.

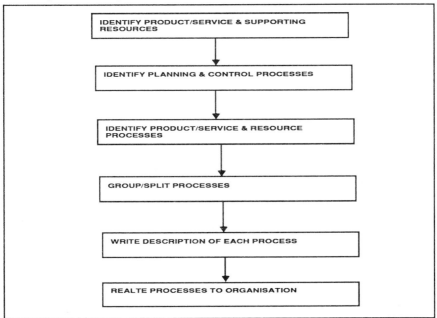

Figure 3.2 : Process of Defining Business Processes

I have outline below some guidelines for defining the Business processes :-

- Look at what is done, what decisions are made, and what resource(s) are managed;

- Look to the Resource Life Cycle stages to identify the processes;

- Classify decisions and/or actions required to perform the work and manage the resource(s);

- Use a verb-object naming syntax to name processes;

- Do not use "and" or "or" names;

- Define processes clearly in one or two sentences. "And" or "or" words should be considered carefully;

- Processes which are relevant to multiple functions can be placed in the common management and administration functional area (eg. plan people resources), unless a better relationship can be found;

- Expect 4 to 10 processes per functional areas/resource.

The Resource Life Cycle stages are as follows :-

- **Requirements** - Decisions or activities that determine <u>what</u> and <u>how much</u> of a product or resource is required. The <u>plan</u> for getting the product or resource, and <u>measurement</u> and <u>control</u> against the plan. Requirements have the following decisions to be made about them :-
  * need;
  * cost;
  * affordability;
  * who does it;
  * who decides.

- **Acquisition** - Decisions or activities performed to develop a product or acquire resources. Acquisitions have the following decisions to be made about them :-
  * how;
  * when;
  * from where;
  * who does it;
  * who decides.

- **Stewardship** - Decisions or activities to maintain status or keep track of products or

resources. Stewardship have the following decisions to be made about them :-
* inventory;
* protect;
* maintain;
* who does it;
* who decides.

- **Disposition** - Decisions or activities that terminate the responsibility of the organisation for a product or end the use of a resource. Dispositions have the following decisions to be made about them :-
  * what;
  * when;
  * how;
  * who does it;
  * who decides.

As a result of the steps illustrated in Figure 3.2, the following may be expected :-

- A list of business processes, typically from 30 to 60, and a description of each process;

- A matrix of processes versus organisation functional areas;

- An understanding of the operations, management and control of the organisation.

If an organisation deems that it is necessary to produce a finer- grained understanding of its business, then the business processes will themselves be analysed and decomposed into business activities.

3.5.   DEVELOP PRELIMINARY BUSINESS DATA MODEL

The defining of business data involves the identification of entities - things that are significant to the business, and the grouping of these entities into logically related categories, called subject data groups. This latter process helps the business develop databases overtime with a minimum of redundancy, and in a manner that allows information systems to be added without major revision to the databases.

A business entity is something of lasting interest to an organisation, that can be uniquely identified and about which the organisation can collect data. Entities may be internal or external to an organisation, and can be categorized as one of the
following :-

- Person, eg Employee;

- Place, eg Restaurant;

- Thing, eg Product;

- Concept, eg Purchase Order;

- Event, eg Sale.

The process for identifying Data Entities which are independent, is as follows :-

- Are they central or essential to this enterprise?

- Are they easily uniquely identified?

- Do they have a stand alone existence?

- Do they have multiple attributes?

The process for identifying Data Entities connoting major business events or transactions, is as follows :-

- Are the events or transactions central or essential to the existence of the enterprise?

- Are they uniquely identified?

- Are they independent or dependent only on the independent entities?

After identifying an initial set of entities, the study team will review the list and combine and/or split entities as necessary to arrive at a comprehensive number.

The Entity List in its own right is useful, but it must be understood that entities have relationships with each other, and in some cases with themselves ! These relationships may be permanent and unchangeable, or they may be temporary or transient. The study team will identify all the relationships that exist between the entities in the entity list, and will produce an Entity-Relationship Diagram/Model. The diagramming technique used will vary from organisation to organisation.

Next the study team identify what data is created by each business process. To do this, a data usage analysis sheet will be documented for each process. In addition, the types of data that are used to perform the process and the types of the data the process generates, will be identified. This phase forces a clarification of business entities, such that omissions and inconsistencies become readily apparent. A matrix of the relationship between the processes and the data entities will be produced.

The knowledge of the relationships of the entities to the processes leads directly to the identification of subject data groups. A Subject Data Group is a natural grouping of entities, which relate to an area of business subjects, as opposed to computer applications.

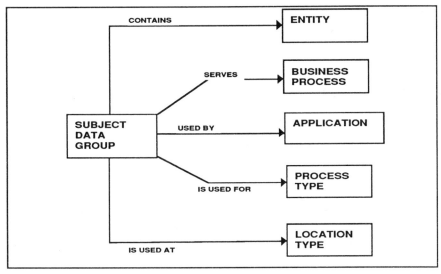

Figure 3.3 : Subject Data Groups

The process for defining Subject Data Groups is as follows :-

- Review the Data Entity Diagram for groupings;

- Review Affinity Analysis;

- Define candidate Subject Data Groups;

- Relate Entities to candidate Subject Data Groups;

- Define Subject Data Groups.

3.6. EVALUATION OF CURRENT SYSTEMS SUPPORT

Up to this phase, the IRP study team has been developing a new perspective of the business by looking at the business in terms of business processes and the subject data groups necessary to support them. Now the team must develop a firm understanding of how data processing currently supports the business, in order to develop recommendations for future actions. This survey will identify how well the current systems support the processes of the organisation, and in addition identify the use of current data. Besides systems that have already been developed, the current developments in data processing must be analysed.

The process for developing the Application Architecture is as follows :-

- Derive Applications;

- Develop Application Portfolio sorted by data priority;

- Review present applications;

- Review current applications under development;

- Analyse Application Portfolio according to business realities;

- Determine requirements for Application Plan.

I have outline below a set of guidelines for developing the Application Architecture :-

- Typically, there should be 1 application for every high level Business Process;

- Unless an application supports all location types, assign a separate application for each location type supported;

- Assign a separate application for each Processing Type (or Time Frame) supported;

- Assign application names which are meaningful to both the users and data processing;

- Applications should be implementable within a reasonable time (eg. from 3 to 9 months) using reasonable resources;

The Process Architecture is used to derive a priority for application development. This can be based on the Process Flow or by using a score system.

3.6.1. Review the Current Systems

The objective of this task is to produce a representation of the functional, operational and technical qualities of the current systems as input into the process of creating the operating plans. This review will analyse each and every application that the organisation currently uses for its business and therefore ascertain the overall quality of the current information systems.

For each application the following information must be gathered :-

- System function;

- System dependency;

- Quality of the design and development;

- Quality of the operational and technical support;

- Quality of operational efficiency;

- The functional quality of the information output.

A questionnaire is used to indicate user department response.

3.6.2. Review the Current Developments

The objective of this task is to produce a representation of the functional quality of planned or developing systems for use into the process of creating the operational plans. This review will analyse each and every computer development that the organisation intends to use for its business and therefore ascertain the overall expected quality of its systems under development.

For each development the following information must be obtained :-

- Development function;

- Development dependency;

- Expected quality of the design;

- Expected quality of the operational and technical support;

- Expected quality of the operational efficiency;

- Expected functional quality of the information output.

A questionnaire is used to initiate user department response.

3.7 DEVELOPMENT OF HIGH LEVEL INFORMATION SYSTEMS ARCHITEC-TURE AND IMPLEMENTATION PLAN

Since data is treated as a business resource, the IRP study team will be able to recommend to management the order, in which information systems need to be developed. Selection criteria for determining the priorities will be determined. Information on the potential benefits and the impact on the business, will be gathered. The IRP study team will also gauge the probable solution areas for the systems, as well as their probability of success. These criteria can be used to rank given information systems on a scale of 1 to 10.

From the findings in the previous phase, the IRP study team will be able to formulate recommendations, which will include the following categories :-

- General recommendations;

- Implementation strategies;

- Applications;

- Management systems;

- Follow-on activities.

The Information Systems Architecture will have been identified. The IRP study team will complete its project by preparing a study report and delivering an executive presentation. The purpose of the report and the presentation is to obtain further management commitment and involvement for implementing the recommendations.

This report and presentation should be made to the following :-

- IRP Management Team;

- Data Processing Management;

- Company Planning Committee;

- Key Company Executives;

- Key Data Processing Staff.

The presentation format should be as follows :-

- What is and why do Information Resource Planning;

- Review of the Information Resource Planning procedure;

- Business Perspective;

- Data Processing Perspective;

- Review of the results:-

*   list of functions or resources;
*   sample of Business Model;
*   simplified Data Entity Model;
*   Subject Data Groups;
*   example of Subject Data Groups;
*   Distribution issues identified;
*   simplified Process Flow description;
*   ordered Application Portfolio;
*   Data Administration Plan.

- Human Resource considerations;

- Technology Architecture considerations;

- Recommendations.

The format of the written report should be consistent with being orientated towards Management, thus it should be short, use business terminology and point to details contained in the appendices. These latter should contain the details, and where necessary point to the Data Dictionary and CASE/IPSE tool.

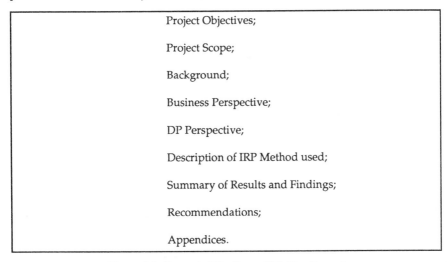

Figure 3.4 : Format of the Formal Written Report

TITLE	MANDITORY/DESIRABLE
Business Model by Function/Resource	M
Business Model by Organisation	M
Data Entity Model	M
Data Entity Detail	D*
Subject Database List	M
Subject Database Detail	D*
Process flow Diagram	M
Source and Use of Data Matrix	M
Ordered Application Portfolio	M
Application Plan	D**
Application Detail	D*
Existing application Findings	D*
Human Resource Planning Considerations	M
Technology Architesture Considerations	M
Distributed Data/Systems findings	M
Data Codification Issues	M
Cost/Benefit Analysis Information	D**
Data Administration Plan	M

*	Available when needed
**	If required by management

Figure 3.5 : Format of the Appendices for the Formal Written Report

FURTHER READING

- Business Systems Planning - Information Systems Planning Guide, IBM, manual GE20-0527-2, 2nd edition, 1978.

- Determining an Organisation's Information Requirements : a State of the Art Survey, S.B.Yadev, Data Base, Spring 1983.

- Information Management and Planning, DATABASE 87, edited by P.Feldman, L.Bhabuta and S.Holloway, Gower Technical Press, 1988.

- A Behavioural Theory of the Firm, R.M.Cyert and J.G.March, Prentice-Hall, 1963.

- Management Information Systems, S.C.Blumenthal, Prentice-Hall, 1969.

- Strategic Planning Methodologies, J.Martin, Prentice-Hall, 1982.

- Introduction to LEAP, LBMS Brochure, 1987.

4. PROJECT MANAGEMENT

4.1 INTRODUCTION

The methodology now reaches the detail stages and from being top-down now becomes bottom-up. It is important that the bottom-up stages should be controlled and planned as much as the top-down stages. A project management and control phase needs to be done first. This should include:-

Budgets   Approved resource time and costs for the whole or the first part of the project.

Deliverables   What should be delivered at specific check points in the project cycle?

Schedules   When activities and tasks should be performed and by whom?

Product Quality Can the deliverables satisfy the requirement? For example : Does a system design document actually contain an acceptable design or does it simply "look" the way it should?

Project management encompasses the functions of budgeting, scheduling and control. Budgeting of Time in a project management environment, is the function of forecasting and allocating people's time (man months or man hours) to certain activities and tasks that are to be performed during the course of a project. Money budgeted is a combination of budgeted time and anticipated individual personnel costs. In project management, both budgeted time and money are equally important. The former is required to tell you how to many people of a particular skill you will need and for what time period to accomplish what task. The latter will tell you what your expenses are likely to be. Scheduling is the function of stating when an activity or task is planned to begin and end. Schedules also indicate the sequences of activities or tasks and the dependencies between them. An activity or task is said to be dependent on another, if it cannot commence until the latter is completed. Control is the function of ensuring an activity or task has been satisfactorily completed. Completion is measured by delivery of an acceptable specified product.

4.2. PLANNING A MAJOR SYSTEMS PROJECT

A major systems development project usually results from an Information Resource Plan. Also the budgeting and schedule for this project should have been identified in this previous stage. Figure 4.1 shows the major check points requiring planning and scheduling.

The starting point in a major systems development project is the output of the Strategic Plan. Unfortunately, this output by itself is not sufficient to plan the project, as it does not clearly indicate the sequence of activities or their dependencies. The activity sequence can be shown using a critical path diagram or a structure diagram or a data flow diagram, to name but a few techniques. DP management must now decide how far ahead to plan the project in detail. This decision will be influenced by the major check points built into the methodology and by other issues such as system complexity, size, forecast project cycle elapsed time, skills and manpower to provide the skills, interfaces external to the system, administrative and computer environments, and the impact of delays or non-delivery of the product on the company.

CHECKPOINT ACTIVITY	ACTIVITIES TO BE BUDGETED AND SCHEDULED IN DETAIL	ACTIVITIES TO BE ESTIMATED
Business Plan	Feasibility Study Review	-
Strategic DP Plan	Define Business Functions Define Corporate Entity Model Define System Implementation Plan Define Migration Strategy Define Hardware/Software Options	-
Detail System Plan	Define System Scope Design Computer System Establish Conversion Files Design forms, Reports and Screens Prepare User Acceptance Plans Prepare System Test Plans Define Test Data Write Procedures and Train Users	Tune Physical DB Code Programs Test Programs Test System User Testing Install Live System Implementation Review System

Figure 4.1 : Major Checkpoints Requiring Panning

The major check points which impact the detailed budgeting and scheduling process are shown in Figure 4.1. The outputs from the check points require approval both from user and DP management. These check points are the least number of breaks in the planning process. If you are developing a larger and more complex system, DP management may choose to increase the number of times approvals are required from the user and DP management to proceed. At each check point, you have the option of refining any estimates that you have made previously.

Having decided on the check points within the methodology for the particular system, the actual detailed planning for activities and tasks should be completed and presented to user and DP management for their approval. The detailed planning should include all tasks to be performed in each activity and the allocation of these tasks to the individuals on the project teams. During this series of planning activities, it should always be kept in mind that people are a very difficult resource to plan and schedule. Skills are not the only criterea that should be considered. Communication problems have been found to increase by a factor of {n(n-1)}/2 as 'n', the team size, increases (1). In other words, merely increasing the number of workers in a project does not necessarily reduce the elapsed time and can in fact increase it. A further consideration is the turnover of staff on a lengthy project. Over one year, you can expect upto 20-25 % turnover, either through reallocation of resources or attrition.

4.3. A PROJECT CONTROL SYSTEM

Project Control Systems can have many and varied requirements. This section describes the basic components of a Project Control System and applies the needs of a 4th Generation methodology to this Project Control System.

4.3.1. Plan Hierarchy

The hierarchy of a project control system generally consists of three levels:-

- A phase level, which is a combination of activities (phases usually occur in a sequence);

- An activity level - The minor activities could be equated to this level;

- A task level - This is the task given to an individual in the project team. More then one individual can be given the same task and each task may also require specific skills.

This hierarchy can be represented by the model shown in Figure 4.2.

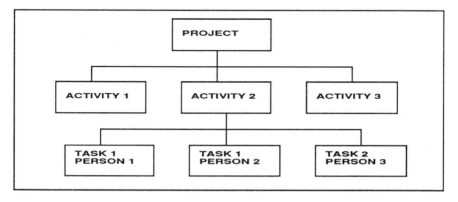

Figure 4.2 : A Project Plan Hierarchy

4.3.2. Dependencies

A dependency implies that a plan, activity or task cannot begin till the phase, activity or task on which it is dependent, is completed. The greater the number of dependencies that are established in a project plan, the more complex it becomes and consequently, the more difficult it is to control. In reality, in a systems design and development environment, very few entities are completely dependent on other entities. Most so- called dependencies disappear when it is found that work can commence on an activity or task using the partially completed output of the working papers that are being produced. In this context it is sufficient to define dependencies at the highest level and to ignore them completely at lower levels.

4.3.3. Project Manpower Organisation

The Project Manpower organisation can be affected by several criterea such as the project's complexity, size, the anticipated elapsed time, the technical and administrative skills required of the staff and the role of the user. This organisation structure will influence the distribution of responsibilities or activities and tasks. In a large project organisation, it is essential that adequate lines of communication be set up between the different teams or groups so that they do not lose sight of the overall project objectives.

4.3.4. Manpower Availability

A project may be planned using two assumptions:-

• An unlimited supply of skilled manpower is always available;

• Only a limited number of skilled staff are available.

The first assumption is generally used when a project has to be completed by a particular date, and you must know how far your available staff can be extended; or you have access to resources outside the company. The second assumption is more common and it applies to the manpower resources you have available in your company.

A further consideration is the fact that staff, though in the office all day, are in fact only available to do productive work associated with the project for much less time. The time they spend working on the project for much less time. The time they spend working on the project is generally referred to as "direct working time", while all other time is called "indirect time". Indirect time includes all training, non-project associated meetings, personal time and so on. Most organisations are fortunate if they can expect their staff to spend seventy to eighty percent of their time on direct work. Hence, all task times should be computed keeping this principle in mind.

In addition to the time loss caused by indirect work, planning should also take into account holidays, sickness and staff turnover. The major cost of this latter piece of indirect work is the learning curve time required to bring new staff to the performance level expected from staff knowledgeable about the project.

4.4. STEPS IN THE DEVELOPMENT OF THE PROJECT PLAN

The planning of the project consists of the following steps:

- **Project Management Initial Step**

  * Use the Structure Diagram output from the Information Resource Plan as a basis and maps out the overall network for the system under development or major upgrade;

  * Identifies the specific outputs to be expected from each major activity;

  * Develops an organisation structure within specific team responsibilities for specific major activities.

- **For Each Team Leader**

  * Identify the specific tasks to be completed within each minor activity;

  * Determine the skills required to complete these tasks;

  * Plan the execution of these tasks using either the resources allocated to them or assume an unlimited pool of resources (also take into account "direct time" availability);

  * Establish a PERT network and a schedule commencing from day one indicating when the minor and major activities should be completed (also indicates what "measurement" is to be used to assure completion of the tasks and minor activities).

- **Project Management Final Step**

  * Superimposes the elapsed time for each major activity provided by the team leaders on the overall systems network and establishes a critical path for the project;

  * Identifies the major check points when approval will be required from DP and user management;

This final project critical path should be re-worked and refined before the project begins. It should be updated at the convenient milestones during the course of the project. The review milestones could be defined as constant time periods such as "once a week" or on completion of specific major activities.

The total management budget in time and money may be obtained by adding up the individual's time and relating it to the individual's costs.

Planning at Task level should be used when detailed planning is required. When overall estimating is to be done, it should probably be sufficient to estimate at the major and minor activity levels and not to break the minor activities into tasks.

4.5.   MANAGEMENT INFORMATION REQUIRED FROM THE PROJECT

The following is the least amount of information that DP management should expect in order to control the projects:-

*   An overall systems development network. Team responsibilities for the activities should also be defined.

*   A critical path network of the major activities to cover each stage of design and development. The critical path should commence at day one and proceed through to the end of the plan. The network should also include the dependencies between the major activities.

*   A detailed network of each activity requiring detailed planning showing the tasks to be performed, the individuals allocated to the tasks and the start and finish dates for each task. Each individual's task should include the actual time to be spent on it. This network should also commence at day one for each activity and proceed to completion of the activity.

*   Schedules for each individual on the project.

*   A turnaround document for each individual indicating work by task and work outstanding. The individual should also be able to indicate if the completion date for a particular task should change.

*   Refined project forecast costs should be prepared at each milestone. The refined project forecast costs are the sum of the actual costs incurred and the remaining costs to be incurred. Actual costs are all the manpower costs incurred to date. Remaining costs are all manpower costs not yet incurred.

4.6. ESTIMATING PROGRAMMER PRODUCTIVITY

Programmer productivity can be defined (2) as "the ratio of Delivered Source Lines (DSL) of code to the total effort in man months required to produce the lines of code". DSL of code refers to executable and debug code and not to other programming code.

Coding can be divided into three classes:-

• Less than normal complexity user interface;

• Equal to normal complexity user interface;

• Greater than normal complexity user interface.

From research (2), certain conclusions can be drawn that are shown in Figure 4.3

LESS THAN NORMAL COMPLEXITY	EQUAL TO NORMAL COMPLEXITY	GREATER THAN NORMAL COMPLEXITY
500 DSL.Man/Month	295 DSL/Man Month	124 DSL/Man Month
Or based on a 21 day man month		
23.8 DSL.Man Day	14.0 DSL/Man Day	5.9 DSL/Man Day

Figure 4.3 : Estimates of Programming time

These are average estimates based on subjective criterea. The use of a 4th Generation Language will reduce these estimates. It is important to remember that these criterea apply only to coders. The manpower estimates should also include the administrative and management costs that accompany the coding costs.

4.7. RULES FOR PROJECT MANAGEMENT

The following golden rules for project management (3) are worth keeping in mind when planning and controlling a systems development project :-

• The systems development team must actively study areas of potential information systems development and evaluate them with respect to their relative overall benefit to the organisation.

• No project shall be planned to last more than six months nor involve more than ten team members. If there is a possibility that either or both could occur, break the project into smaller projects.

- The best practical systems should be allowed to develop through users participation in refining the emerging system, providing always that close cost monitoring is employed to avoid flights of fancy.

- Cost and time scale estimates must only be given in a phased basis. It is pointless to commit to any guaranteed price or time scale until it is clear what is being produced in each unit of development.

- User management must be persuaded of the cost and the value of the releasing key personnel to be involved in the systems development process.

- It is no use expecting creative system development staff to act as pen-pushing form fillers. Good progress monitoring will only be achieved by simple reporting methods, and good documentation as a by-product of the development method itself.

- The project manager must regard it as a matter of priority to maintain an awareness of what needs to be scheduled and any factors preventing planned progress.

- A well planned program of education and training for the eventual users of the system will save a great deal of money on unnecessary support later.

- The project manager must ensure that adequate documentation at the required standard is made available for the system to be supported and enhanced in the future, and that the system itself be structured for ease of maintenance and enhancement.

- Improved development techniques can only be achieved through a program of staff development, which begins with the project managers identifying the training needs of individual staff.

4.8.   PROJECT CONTROL FOR MAINTENANCE

Budgeting, scheduling and controlling maintenance and minor system enhancements should not be handled in the same manner as a major project. This is because maintenance and minor enhancement have short time frames between identification of the problem and its resolution. A common sense approach is to either allocate a certain percentage of staff time on a continuing basis to maintenance or to make one or more personnel responsible for this function only. The scheduling and controlling of tasks associated with maintenance or minor system modifications could similarly be simplified by classifying all such tasks as either "investigations" or as "actions taken".

REFERENCES

1. THE MYTHICAL MAN MONTH: ESSAYS ON SOFTWARE ENGINEERING,
    F.P. Brooks Jr., Addison-Weasley, 1975

2. METHOD OF PROGRAMMING MEASUREMENT AND ESTIMATION,
    C.E. Walston and C.P. Felix, IBM Systems Journal 1/77, January 1977

3. GUIDELINES FOR EFFECTIVE PROJECT MANAGEMENT, P. Haine, Savant
    Institute, 1981.

5. FUNCTIONAL DECOMPOSITION

5.1 INTRODUCTION

Functional analysis has many purposes. The main uses are :-

- To find out the business activities a system must support and hence what programs will be required.

- To refine the entity model

- To design the databases required to support the system, as functional analysis provides quantifiable information on the way the company's data will be used.

- To provide the basis for designing programs.

There are two concepts used in functional analysis, those of function and an event.

5.2. FUNCTIONS

A function is a business activity. It is what the company does in order to operate; for example it pays people, handles orders, deals with enquiries, controls lending, and so on. Strictly speaking these are "functional types" a function occurrence or execution being the payment of a specific person,the handling of a specific order, etc.. A function type is not defined in terms of who performs the function - the same function type can be performed by a number of people and possibly for different purposes. Equally a function is not defined in terms of how its inputs and outputs have been implemented or in terms of machines to be used. A function states what is done and refers only to entity types and attribute types. How the function is to be carried out is decided during a latter design stage.

The three basic rules for determining the definition of a function are:-

- Never mention people or jobs.

- Never mention forms, output reports or other procedural things: Only refer to entity types or attribute types or values.

- Never mention machines, such as computers, typewriters, etc. which are involved in the implementation of the function;.

Several aspects of functions are worth noting:-

- Each function is an action upon something, expressed in terms of a simple declarative statement which consists of a verb and an object. For example, Calculate (verb) interest on a loan (object)

- Every function must involve the transformation of some "input" to some "output" and functions are related by their outputs and inputs; one function producing output that is the input for another function. For example, Figure 5.1 shows the inputs and outputs of some sample functions. Notice that some functions have multiple inputs, and in the case of "packed label goods", its output is part of the input for "deliver goods" function.

INPUT	FUNCTION	OUTPUT
Unpaid people,pay details	PAY PEOPLE	Paid people
Unpacked goods in stock,order details	PACK & LABEL GOODS	Packed labelled goods
Unallocated patient, ward information	ALLOCATE PATIENT TO WARD	Allocated ward patient
Packed & labelelled goods, delivery details,etc	DELIVER GOODS	Delivered goods
Patient booked for operation,operation schedule,doctors,etc	OPERATE ON PATIENT	Patient who has undergone operation

Figure 5.1 : Inputs and Outputs of certain Functions

- It is important that no distinction is made between functions which are physical tasks, clerical functions, and managerial functions, such as decisions. The job in hand is studying the business and how it operates, not just the tasks that may be computerised. The knowledge of the existence of a physical or decision task is as useful as the knowledge of a clerical task in the design of a system, because it helps the analyst to understand the dependencies between functions and the way the business operates.

- Functions may exist which are not executed for every occurrence of their object entities. Such functions are termed optional and the conditions under which they will be executed must be documented. For example, the function "cancel patient's appointments" will be executed only if the patient has appointments. Optional functions depend upon values of attributes and/or the participation in the relationship of their object entities. The use of the word "may" with the verb and/or a condition clause indicates that there is optionality. In the example above, it would be better to describe the function as "may cancel patient's appointments if any exist".

- In many cases any one group of functions may be executed, but not more than one. These are termed exclusive function types. The condition determining the selection of the function for execution must be documented. For example, the functions :-

"handle patient's death if in patient" and

"handle patient's death if out-patient"

are mutually exclusive.

The following points (1) may help in determining what function types a company has:-

- Function types and the organisation of the company are NOT the same. It is dangerous to assume that jobs and divisions in the organisation can be used as a basis functional analysis.

- If a procedure manual for an area under study is available, this will often specify many of the functions which are completed in the area. These are usually found within the description of active verbs describing things that are done.

- Functions sometimes produce tangible end-products. It is therefore often useful to understand what the end-products of each function type in the area under study are. An end-product should not be confused with reports or documents presently being produced; it means the known necessary outputs of the overall function, such as a priced, validated and edited order as a result of the "handle order" function.

- Since events are triggers to functions, the events should be used as a prompt for the user, to make sure all the functions have been covered.

5.3. EVENTS

An Event is the stimulus or trigger which initiates one or more functions. Every function is triggered by an event, even if it is only the simple event of the preceding function having been completed. Events are of interest because:

- They are used in determining the programs required in the system.

- They help to identify the functions of the company.

The events of interest for system/program design are events which start or initiate a chain of functions. Those events which mark the expected completion of one function and hence the start of the next are of less interest. In Figure 5.2 some examples are given of initiating events.

Person dies	an external event
Patient books appointment	an external event
Operation completed	an internal. physical event
Month-end	an internal, time-dependent event
Person's medicine changed	an internal event, based on decision

Figure 5.2 : Examples of Events of Interest

Events are either :-

- External to the area under study, ie. not generated by the business operations of the particular part of the business being studied,

or

- Internal to the area, ie. generated by the business activities under study, and dependent upon the situation fully relevant to the part of the business. These situations are likely to be the success or otherwise of a previous function, a managerial decision or a specific time being reached.

The relationship between functions and events is quite complex. An event can be initiate more than one function, and in turn a function can be initiated by more than one event.

In order to determine events the following questions (1) can be useful:-

- Which events can cause an entity to "die" or become of no further importance to the company?

- Which events cause an entity to be "born"?

- Which events cause a change in the values of each attribute of an entity?

- Which events cause a change in the relationship between entities, ie establish the relationships or break them?

It is also useful to bear in mind the following points (1) when considering events:-

- Inquiries and decisions are events.

- Events can be regular - month-end, or irregular - person admitted to hospital.

- Events can be predictable - operation completed, or unpredictable - person dies.

- Events can be normal - patient arrives for an appointment, or exceptional - patient fails to attend an appointment.

5.4.   FUNCTIONAL DECOMPOSITION

A business can be viewed as a single function which can be divided into a hierarchy of sets of lower level functions. Thus the highest level function of a Bank is likely to be Banking, and the sub-functions could be Lending, Borrowing, Customer servicing and Money Management. This progressive analysis of functions into more detailed functions is termed "functional decomposition". It allows the functions of a company to be described from the highest possible functional level to the most detailed level required, using a single technique and format. Functional decomposition has several purposes:-

- It ensures that the analyst completely understands the business and the business activities before any design takes place.

- The results of functional decomposition are used for system/program design and in determining the dataviews needed, and hence the data needed.

As with entity models the results of functional analysis, including functional decomposition are documented using diagrams and supplemented with entries to the data dictionary for additional information. The diagrammatic conventions used for functional decomposition are shown in Figure 5.3. An event is represented by an arrow, and a function by a box in which the name of the function is written.

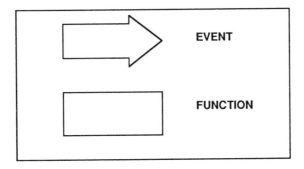

Figure 5.3 : Diagrammatic Conventions for Functional Decomposition

The function hierarchy shown in figure 5.4 shows how the functions are related when decomposed. Function A is composed of subfunctions B, C and D; Function D consists of subfunctions E, F and G.

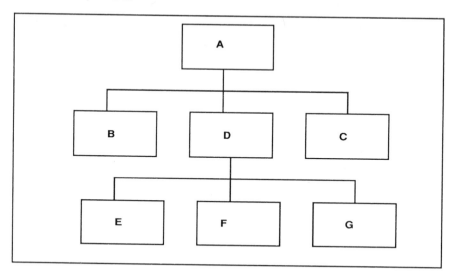

Figure 5.4 : Function Hierarchy Diagram

Where a function consists of subfunction which is repeated several times, the diagrammatic conventions are shown in Figure 5.5. In the example, Function A consists of function B repeated several times.

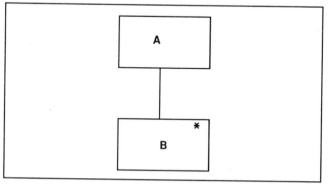

Figure 5.5 : Diagrammatic Conventions for Functional Decomposition Iteration

Where functions are selectable, the diagrammatic convention is as shown in Figures 5.6 and

5.8. In Figure 5.7 example, an occurrence of Function A consists either of B or C - exclusive.

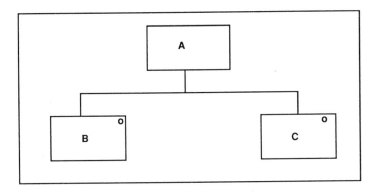

Figure 5.6 : Function Hierarchy Diagram Showing Exclusivity

In Figure 5.7 example, Function A consists of B and may also consist of C - optional.

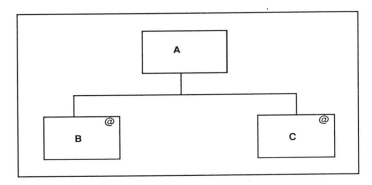

Figure 5.7 : Function Hierarchy Diagram Showing Optionality

The best way to describe functional decomposition is to use an everyday example to demonstrate the principles. Functional decomposition is a "top down" method of analysing what a business does. The first step is therefore to determine what is the top level function of the area under study and then proceed towards greater detail. In figure 5.8, the top level function in the example is that of household management, composed of the subfunctions of shopping, entertaining, washing, cleaning and so on. The highest level function has been broken down into all subordinate tasks which must be performed in order to complete it.

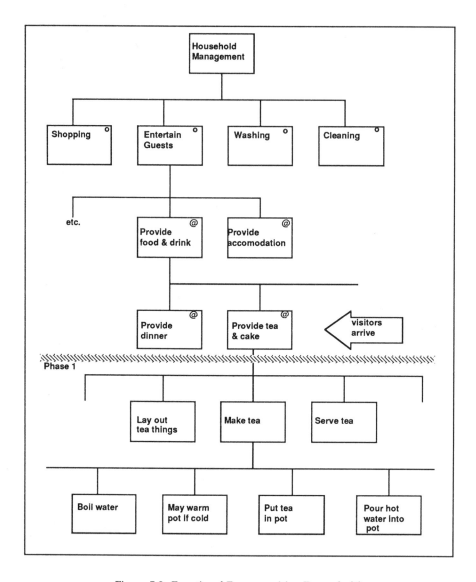

Figure 5.8 : Functional Decomposition Example (1)

At the next level in the example, the task of "entertain guests" is broken down further. In order to entertain guests, the tasks of providing tea are undertaken. As each function is decomposed the tasks become more and more detailed and specific. It is also possible at the lowest levels in the hierarchy to specify the events which start the function. For example, the function "provide tea/cakes" can be triggered by the event "visitor's arrive".

Seven points to understand are:-

- Each function in the hierarchy is the sum of its subfunctions. A function cannot include subfunctions which are not described or whose meaning is not conveyed by the function name or definition. For example, "make tea" could not include "make cakes".

- A function must be broken down into more than one subfunction. For example, "provide tea" could not have consisted of one task, "make tea".

- Functions can occur quite legitimately in more than one hierarchy. The function "boil water" may also occur within the hierarchy whose main function is "provide dinner". This commonality of functions is especially important in the design of systems and programs as it can indicate where one process could be used to implement more than one function and also where common programs or modules can be used.

- The completion of one function in one hierarchy may be the event which triggers off a series of functions in another hierarchy. For example, the function "buying the ingredients" within the shopping hierarchy may have to be completed before the function "make cakes" can start.

- At the highest level, a business will often describe the functions using the present participle of a verb together with an object, eg. washing (omitted object - linen). At this level, there will be no sequence to the functions as this form of verb construct is used to imply continuous or on-going activity. Once the function can be related to an event, the verb is used in imperative mode denoting action and the sequence of functions, wherever there is a sequence, can be shown. For example, the event "visitor's arrive" triggers "provide tea/cakes".

- There is a danger of defining functions as if one were defining a batch system. This is known as the 'batching trap' and must be avoided, as it can lead to the creation of unnecessary transactions and badly designed programs. The batching trap can also be found in organisations. For instance, if responsibilities have been split between two people for what is one task, it may appear to be two, because of the artificial job split.

- It may seem an obvious point, but it is worth stating, that only those functions which are relevant to the purposes of the study should be decomposed to any level of detail.

The main advantage of functional decomposition is that the levels of detail can be geared to the stage reached in the project or to the purposes of the project. The first stage of the project is often "user requirements", which require a broad indication of what the requirements of the users are in terms of functions in order that the users can agree on them and decide priorities before the next stage is started. Functional decomposition would thus be completed down to the level required, probably the top three to four levels in the hierarchy. In Figure 5.9 , this is represented by Phase 1. The next stage might be used for system design. At this stage in the project, the function hierarchy would be decomposed further until enough information was known to enable the system to be designed. At this stage, a decision would be made as to which functions were to be computerised and which were not and what were the priorities. In Figure 5.8 this would roughly equate to phase 2. At this stage the elementary functions will have been established. This is a function for which it would be better to decompose further using Structured English descriptions.

Functional decomposition has many advantages over the traditional English language text approach. Text is always one-dimensional. All the detail has to be forced into the same paragraphs and sentences as the text which give the overall picture and 'sets the scene'. The detail cannot be expanded progressively within the text, and the description usually has to be rewritten, if more information needs to be added.

5.5. DATA FLOW DIAGRAMS

Data Flow Diagrams are used to show the sequencing of functions for each event, their dependencies and where parallel activities can occur. In many methodologies, it is usual to complete the data flow diagrams for each level in the function hierarchy in parallel with functional decomposition. The purposes of the Data Flow Diagram are:-

•   To ensure that the function hierarchy is complete and that no functions have been omitted or placed at the wrong level.

•   To provide a basis for system and program design by showing the order of processing which must be completed for each translation.

In Figure 5.9, the various basic diagrammatic conventions used to draw data flow diagrams by different methodologies are shown.

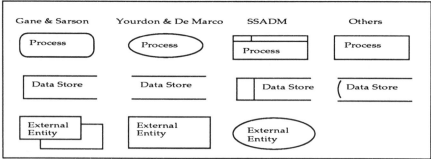

Figure 5.9 : Symbols for Data Flow Diagram

Data flow diagrams can be drawn for each level of the function hierarchy. The functions at that level are shown in a logical sequence from left to right in the diagram by considering, firstly the events which have triggered the functions, and secondly the input and output of the function. Each event is identified to a function and the following questions asked about each function:-

•   What function must be complete before this function?

•   What functions can be completed at the same time as this function?

•   What functions cannot start until after this function is completed?

It is important that every event is followed through to its logical conclusion to ensure that functions have not been missed. Each function must now be examined to ensure that the output produced by one function is the input used by the next function in the sequence. If this is not the case, either a function has been missed, or the sequence is wrong, or the levels in the hierarchy have been wrongly defined.

REFERENCES

1. DATA ANALYSIS, R. Rock-Evans, IPC Electrical-Electronic Press Ltd, 1981.

6. PROTOTYPING WITH FOURTH GENERATION ENVIRONMENT TOOLS

6.1 INTRODUCTION

Prototyping has been defined as the process of building and refining a working model of the final operational system during the development process. The main purpose of prototyping is to refine functions, inputs and outputs of the system during the design phase without having to wait for development to be completed. Prototyping is not a substitute for good analysis and design, nor is it an excuse to abandon proven structured design techniques, adequate documentation or good structured programming techniques. If used properly, prototyping can be an effective tool and an aid in developing systems that allows closer user participation in the design process, leading to systems that meet the needs of users.

In its simplest form a prototype can be nothing more than a mock- up of system outputs. Sample reports and screen layouts are developed and hardcopy representations are reviewed with the user. These will eventually become part of of the detailed system specification. For this, almost any interactive programming tool that allows an analyst to design mock-ups interactively and then produce hardcopies, can be used.

A more elaborate form of prototype is a throw-away functional model of the proposed system. This type simulates the functionality of the proposed system. Users can actually sit at a terminal an use the system as it would be used in its final form. A limitation of this method is that it is still purely a model not capable of evolving into the final operational system. However, it is excellent for demonstrating the system and selling it to management. The prototype can serve as a useful requirements tool to communicate the systems specification to the application developers. For a throw-away functional model, any interactive software tool capable of simulating a real system is adequate, as long as it can produce a model fairly quickly. PC products are often used to produce these prototypes.

The third prototyping method, called an evolutionary system, has all the attributes of the throw-away with the additional capability of evolving into the final system.

Figure 6.1 shows the two main prototyping choices - the throw-away model and the evolutionary model approaches (1).

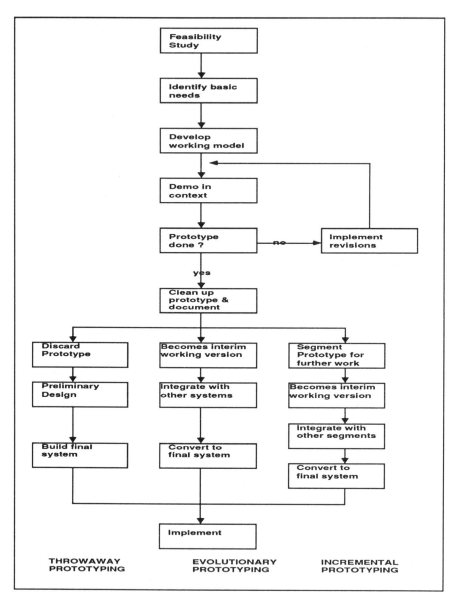

Figure 6.1 : Types of Prototyping

Prototyping can be regarded in several different ways:

- A means of concentrating a user's ideas by presenting them back to him as they would appear when fully developed, but as part of an iterative cycle of refining the actual requirements,

- A means of automatically documenting a system as described by a user, and of gaining a users commitment to stabilizing his requirements,

- A means of producing a 'cheap-and-cheerful' working system which can be re-written for greater efficiency at a later date,

- A staged evolution of a system from initial concept to a complete, working, operational version.

Depending on the tools available, prototyping can be a mix of any or all of these views. The minimum requirements for accepting a system into the operational cycle of an organisation should be that both the data structure and generated code conform to the site's standards and quality assurance testing. An experienced DP professional who has worked within the organisation for some time may well reach the stage where the output from his prototyping stage needs little refinement to meet the standards set. This is where the skill factor will continue to play an important role, despite the apparent 'deskilling' influence of 4th Generation Environment.

Probably the most important role of prototyping is the process of defining user requirements by building and refining a working model, this should not, however, preclude the possibility of using all or part of this working model in the finally developed system, provided that the various site standards are maintained.

6.2.   THE CASE FOR PROTOTYPING

A large number of problems related to systems design and development have surfaced which make the approach of prototyping an absolute necessity. These problems include:-

- People Costs versus Computer Costs

- Application Back Log

- Increases in development and Programming Productivity

- Faster turnaround for more sophisticated systems

- Not enough skilled programmers

- Program detail

- Inadequate documentation

6.2.1. People Costs versus Computer Costs

The cost of generating one hundred thousand instructions has fallen from 1.26 in 1952 to seven tenths of a cent in 1980 (2), while people costs are rising at ten percent. Hence it is imperative that the people share of the total development cost be reduced to as low as possible.

6.2.2 Application Backlog

Many large organisations have a two to five year application backlog.. This backlog is not a large number of equal projects or tasks; it is a very diverse three-dimensional workload. The first dimensions of the application backlog is different types of applications. They range all the way from large scale systems to ad-hoc requests. This is not not a complete list.

- New commercial systems - are the large live applications which are the bread and butter systems automating an organisation's basic business service.

- Systems Enhancements is a polite phrase for maintenance. This is the predominant programming activity today, occupying the lion' share of DP's time budget. Again, most of this activity is done for large scale applications and often represents actual enhancements as opposed to fixes of the problems.

- Departmental systems are applications that an end user may have had in a desk drawer on cards. In the past, these applications simply were not important enough to get into the work queue of DP. They are a primary factor behind the proliferation of Personal Computers in companies today.

- One time requests are ad-hoc queries and reports generally used for senior or middle management decision making.

- The invisible backlog represents all the applications that are needed to be developed but have not been requested yet because users are still waiting for work to finish on other applications.

Also, applications often have very complex routines, perhaps high volume updating requirements, as well as more simple information retrieval requirements. The third dimension on the application backlog is the traditional software life cycle. Some fourth generation products seem to have an unwritten philosophy that says "When you step up to the fourth generation, you do not need to plan what you do anymore. Just start coding". Fourth generation technology doe not do away with design and planning. It should however offer facilities to make design and planning more productive.

6.2.3 Increases in Development and Programming Productivity

Martin (3) states that the maximum increase in development and programming using the structured techniques over techniques that are not structured, is 25 %. This increased productivity is nowhere near sufficient to cope with anticipated demand.

6.2.4. Faster Turnaround for More Sophisticated Systems

Users are demanding a shorter development life cycle and systems which more accurately reflect their needs so that anticipated benefits can be realised early.

6.2.5. Not Enough Skilled Programmers

The increased demand for effective programmers is making them a scarce and expensive commodity.

6.2.6. Program Detail

Design errors that result from poorly understood or poorly defined specifications are costly and time consuming to fix later on. A SHARE study (2) has indicated that one third of development time is spent on logic, while two thirds of the effort are spent on handling systems functions such as operating systems, database or TP. Hence a reduction in the effort spent on these systems functions could result in real savings.

6.2.7. Inadequate Documentation

It is a common experience to fix one bug in a program and to create two more. This generally results from inadequate documentation and the fact that each programmer or analyst for that matter is an individual and tend to write/code in their own way, which cannot be completely understood or followed by anyone else.

6.3. THE ADVANTAGES OF PROTOTYPING

Prototyping using a fourth generation tools has the following advantages which to a greater extent reduce the problems described in the previous section :-

- Increased programmer Productivity - IBM states that their experience with users using Application Generators has shown increases in programmer productivity in the range of 5 to 15 times (2).

- Working Model versus a Paper Model - The user has a working model of the system to test instead of a paper model such as data flow diagrams. As a result, he can modify his requirements after seeing how the prototype system functions. With conventional systems analysis and design, the user sees a working system only after the system is ready for implementation and changes to requirements cannot be incorporated till much later.

- Model Iterations - As the prototype has been developed with minimal effort, changes can be made quickly and the model can proceed through several iterations before it is approved for use by the user.

- User specification is not frozen - The user specification is not frozen as in conventional systems, as the system itself can be changed easily at any time.

- Production of Error Free Programs - All programming languages have specific rules and regulations which control the internal consistency of the language compiler. As such, it is very easy to miss some obscure punctuation mark or other requirement which can result in several tests and recompiles. In general, most application generator programs are self-documenting and provide all relevant information about the program logic, data referenced, etc.

- Maintenance and Enhancement - program maintenance and enhancement is greatly simplified as only logic functions and not systems functions are effected (4).

- Systems performance - One of the primary reasons quoted by DP personnel for not using application generators is reduced systems performance. In other words they believe that most application generators have slow response times and consume large amounts of computer core. Martin states that this is untrue and illustrates this with IBM's DMS, which takes one-sixth of the compiled time for the same functions written in COBOL, as it generates major blocks of code which are precompiled (3). This conclusion is supported by Dalton after experience with application generators (4).

6.4.   INITIAL REQUIREMENTS

Before any prototyping can be carried out, a minimum number of requirements must have been fulfilled. These will include:

- Awareness of the software tools which are to be used, and an understanding of what they are or are not capable of achieving.

- From the Information Resource Plan (or if this has not yet been completed, from the initial system requirements), the scope of the system to be implemented and an initial (simplified) data model.

- A table of sub-functions split into online updates, online retrieval, batch updates, standard reports, and online end-user facilities.

- The agreement of the end-users to the method of progressing, and acceptance of the involvement required on their part.

6.5. PROTOTYPING SCREENS AND INTER-SCREEN FLOW

About the one thing that most 4th Generation Environment packages have in common is the ability to define online screens interactively, and display them back to an end user for refinement with editors of greater or lesser sophistication. Some more advanced packages permit a full facsimile of screens developed in this way, allowing the end-user to actually enter values into the screens, with automatic validation of fields according the specification. The user can thus see exactly how the finished system will appear at a very early stage in development.

Of more interest from the analysis point of view, this process gives us a definition of the local view of data as seen by the particular sub-function. This may not be complete at this stage, as validation of fields entered against an existing database table may be required, but at the minimum we are given a list of fields of interest, and part of the design process is to ensure that each field on each screen has an origin somewhere on the database, and is referenced in one or more places by other applications.

Having established the main update and enquiry screens to be used in the application, the flow between the screens also needs to be prototyped. This will normally involve defining one or more further screens which will be selection menus, and either writing or generating a simple program which will invoke the next screen in sequence or return to a previous screen. This also should be developed with assistance from the end-user, and then the whole outward appearance of the application signed off by the user as confirmation that this is the way he wants the system to appear. This is simple to achieve provided that the software permits hardcopies to be taken. Ultimately the control program compilation listing should show not only the logic by which control is passed between screens, but also include facsimile hardcopies of each screen, with definitions of field editing and other relevant information.

During the prototyping process, whenever a particular part of the system has been agreed by the appropriate end-users and 'signed- off', that part of the developed system should be frozen by whatever mechanism the software tools make available, if necessary by moving the relevant parts into a read-only environment. This now becomes a part of the formal system specification.

6.6.   DEFINING STANDARD REPORTS

Provided that the tools are available, standard reports can also be defined interactively, and either facsimilied or produced with the aid of a trivial program. The local dataviews from each report, as with those from the online system prototype, also need to be checked against the data available on the projected database.

6.7.   DEFINING PROCESSING RULES

Regardless of the type of language used within a particular 4th Generation Environment software system, the same basic information needs to be defined for each application. The structure of a program will be determined by the nature of the data controlling it. In most batch update programs the driving force is a transaction file, which will be processed sequentially in its entirety unless an unexpected condition occurs. Online systems are likewise normally driven by a screen input transaction which selects specific occurrences of entities (represented by dataviews). Standard reports and some online interrogation commands are driven by the database, where all the data meeting specified selection criteria are processed in a particular sequence. There are therefore two basic program shells, one representing a transaction driven approach, the other a data driven approach.

Having acquired a selection of data, various validations must be made before applying any updates to the database or presenting details to the report or screen handler.

Some 4th Generation Environment systems take a rigid approach by providing fixed program shells which invoke user-coded routines to handle the exceptions. While this provides extremely fast generation of very simple procedures, more complicated require-ments become progressively more difficult to fit into these shells. A less regimented non-procedural language, in addition to making complex procedures easier to cope with, may be used at an early stage to document the processing requirements of an application, later to be evolved into the actual operational program.

An example of a transaction driven approach follows, using Applied Data Research's IDEAL product as an example:

First Attempt

```
<<NEW-ORDER>> PROCEDURE
LOOP
TRANSMIT ORDER-SCREEN          :DISPLAY ORDER-DETAIL SCREEN
UNTIL ORDER-NO = 0             :USE ORDER NO 0 TO END RUN
DO VALIDATE-CUSTOMER           :CHECK CUSTOMER EXISTS AND
                              :IS WITHIN CREDIT LIMIT
DO VALIDATE-PART               :CHECK VALID PART NO
DO CHECK-STOCK                 :SEE IF PART IN STOCK
IF NO-STOCK
DO PLACE-FACTORY-ORDER         :RAISE WORKS ORDER ON MANUF. SYS
ELSE
DO STOCK-WITHDRAWAL            :DECREMENT STOCK COUNT
ENDIF
DO ORDER-ACKNOWLEDGE           :RAISE PAPERWORK FOR DISPATCH
ENDLOOP
ENDPROCEDURE
```

This program structure, while capable of being compiled under ADR/IDEAL 4th Generation Environment system, is equally suitable for presenting to an end user, and together with a hard- copy of the appropriate screen will permit mistakes to be rectified while retaining full documentation of the requirements.

In this instance it would probably be pointed out that an order may consist of up to 10 detail lines, and the functional description modified as follows:

Modified Structure

```
<<NEW-ORDER>> PROCEDURE
LOOP
TRANSMIT ORDER-SCREEN          :DISPLAY ORDER-DETAIL SCREEN
UNTIL ORDER-NO = 0             :USER ORDER NO 0 TO END RUN
DO VALIDATE CUSTOMER           :CHECK CUSTOMER EXISTS AND
                              :IS WITHIN CREDIT LIMIT
DO PROCESS-ORDER-LINES         :HANDLE UP TO 10 LINES PER ORDER
DO ORDER-ACKNOWLEDGE           :RAISE PAPERWORK FOR DISPATCH
ENDLOOP
ENDPROCEDURE
<<PROCESS-ORDER-LINES>> PROCEDURE
LOOP VARYING COUNT FROM 1 BY 1 UP THROUGH 10
                              :THIS LOOP PROCESSES EACH LINE IN
                              :TURN UNTIL EITHER NO MORE LINES
                              :HAVE BEEN ENTERED OR 10 LINES
                              :HAVE BEEN PROCESSED
UNTIL PART-NO(COUNT) = 0
DO VALIDATE-PART               :CHECK VALID PART-NO
DO CHECK-STOCK                 :SEE IF PART IN STOCK
IF NO-STOCK
DO PLACE-FACTORY-ORDER         :RAISE WORKS-ORDER ON MANUF. SYS
ELSE
DO STOCK-WITHDRAWAL            :DECREMENT STOCK COUNT
ENDIF
ENDLOOP
ENDPROCEDURE
```

Once the basic shell of the program is acceptable to the user, each procedure named within it can be progressively expanded to accommodate all required validation, database updates, and reporting. By using this very structured pseudo-code an end user who understands his own system, but who would have no idea how to go about describing his requirements to a DP professional, can be driven progressively through the system design, and can contribute at each stage.

After each major change or addition to the specification, a new version (or copy) of the functional description should be started so as to provide a way to return to a known point if an error has been made.

Gradually the specification actually becomes the source code for the application, leaving only the lowest level calculations and subroutines to be coded.

As the user will have contributed to every stage of the development process there is little chance for misinterpretation of requirements to creep in, resulting not only in a system which performs in the way the user wants, but also a method which often highlights areas in which a users own concept of the system fails to tie up with reality when demonstrated through a prototype.

At each stage in the design process, the system prototype should be demonstrated in its entirety to the appropriate users, and 'signed-off' as correct before starting any further phase. In order to make a more realistic presentation during the stages before the database design is completed, it is possible to code test data into the prototype programs in the form of Working Data (similar to Working Storage in Cobol). The Working Data developed in this way as part of the prototyping approach has a double value, since it also serves to confirm the requirements of the local dataviews required by the program. Equally with some products it is possible to dynamically define files and populate using simple add programs. An example of a product that uses the latter approach is Cincom's MANTIS.

6.8. ITERATIVE SYSTEMS REQUIREMENTS DESIGN

To develop information systems in the 4th Generation environment using a Relational Database Management System we need to combine various techniques together to exploit the environment. So to produce a Conceptual Model as well as a functionally complete system, the following actions should be done :-

- Define the detailed scope of the chosen system/project - this is done using the Information Resource Plan deliverables as the base and looking at the feasibility of the system/project in terms of time, man-power and cost.

- Identify the services, the inputs and the outputs with the user - this is done using the prototyping method described above, whilst still following structured design principles.

- The names and meaning of the data items and entities must be established - this done by Data Administration ensuring that there is a naming convention, preferably one that is enforceable automatically.

- Once the System Prototype has been agreed with the user, the screens, reports, working data and parameter data can be used as the user views of data for the normalisation techniques described in chapter n.

- Canonical Synthesis - this is the process of combining all the normalised views of data from the previous step to produce the simplest set of tables, necessary to support the users needs for the given system or project.

- There is a second Canonical Synthesis process that has to be carried out before physical design. In this the Conceptual Data Model produced from the previous step is merged with the Company Conceptual Data Model. This process helps in identifying changes to the company model as well as possible conflict areas with existing or potential systems and their usage of the data.

REFERENCES

1. SHORTCUT TO SYSTEM DESIGN, A. Bernstein, Business Computer Systems, June 1985.

2. APPLICATION DEVELOPMENT PRODUCTIVITY, D. Davis, IBM Corporation, GUIDE 51, Session SD-16, August 1980.

3. APPLICATION DEVELOPMENT WITHOUT PROGRAMMERS, J. Martin, Prentice-Hall Inc., 1982.

4. OPEN SYSTEMS - ARE PROGRAMMERS REALLY NECESSARY, R. Dalton, Open Systems, 1981.

FURTHER READING

- Application Prototyping : A requirement definition strategy for the 80's, B.H.Boar, Wiley, 1984.

- The Prototyping Methodology, K.E.Lantz, Prentice-Hall.

- Prototyping Systems and Application Productivity, Xephon Consultancy Report, 1985.

- Software Prototyping in the 80's, D.C.Ince and S.Hehsmatpour, Dept. of Computing Open University, 1987.

- Building Applications using a 4GL, 2nd Edition, M.G.Sobell, Sobell Assoicates Inc. 1986.

- Prototyping Information Systems, W.C.Andrews, Journals of System Management, vol 34, Sept 1983.

- Prototyping : giving users a working model for application development, B.H.Boar, Computer World, vol 17, Sept 1983.

7. NORMALISATION

7.1 INTRODUCTION

Normalisation is a step-by step process for replacing associations between data in hierarchical or network form with associations in a two-dimensional flat tabular form. The tables have to be set up in such a way that no information about associations between data items is lost.

7.2 NORMALISATION TERMS

There are a number of terms associated with the subject that need explaining; they are as outlined below.

7.2.1 Relation

A Relation is the name given to the two dimensional table of data items describing one data type or entity type (eg. Customer). Relations have the following properties:-

- Each column in the table represents one elementary data item also referred to as an attribute of the Relation. There are no repeating groups in a relation.

- In any column all the values that occur are of the same kind.

- Each column is assigned a distinct name, referred to as the Attribute name.

- All rows are distinct; duplicate rows are not allowed.

- Both the rows and the columns can be viewed in any sequence without affecting either the information content or the semantics of any function using the table, ie. the row order and the column order are of no significance in describing the relation.

7.2.2 Tuple

A tuple is a group of related data items or Attributes. A relation is a set of tuples.

7.2.3 Attribute

An attribute is an elementary data item that functionally describes a given data type. A complete set of these attributes describing a given data type form the Relation for that data type.

7.2.4 Domain

A Domain is a collection of all possible values for the elementary data items of the same type in a Relation. From this set of values the Attribute(s) draw the actual values.

7.2.5. Data Type

A data type or entity type is a major functional item of the company, eg. Customer.

7.3.   EXAMPLE OF A RELATION

Figure 7.1 shows an example of a relation. It has been given the name CUSTOMER. The relation describes the data type or entity type also known as CUSTOMER. There are 3 points to remember :-

•   A relation is equivalent to a table.

•   A tuple is equivalent to a record.

•   An attribute is equivalent to an elementary field.

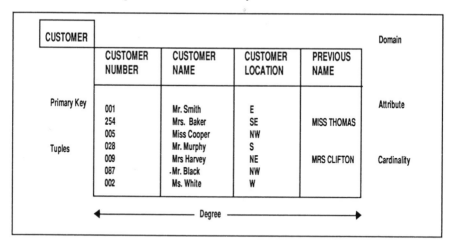

Figure 7.1 : An Example of a Relation

It is important to note the following :-

- No duplicate tuples (no null, unique key)

- Order top-to-bottom is of no significance

- Order left-to-right is of no significance.

- All attributes are elementary.

- All attribute values are drawn from the Domain.

7.4. THE NORMAL FORMS

There have been two distinct aspects to the development of the relational database idea: That concerned with the conventions and operations to enable practical software to be constructed, and that to provide a "theory of data" which will assist in good database design for making use of such software.

The "theory of data" approach has led to understandings and to practical database design methods which do not depend on the existence of relational database software and "Normalisation" has become part of the standard toolkit of techniques of most database designers. Given an appropriate relational database design for a particular situation then this can be mapped onto the facilities of the particular database management system product being used. The logical database design can be implemented directly using a relational database management system, but requires a further phase of refinement to permit it to be implemented on any other type.

7.4.1. First Normal Form

In this section, we discuss the basic ideas of normalisation. It should be appreciated that the ideas behind second, third and further normal forms are different in character from that of first normal form:

A relation is in FIRST NORMAL FORM if each of its attributes is defined over a domain of elementary values.

This definition of first normal form prevents an attribute from taking sets as values (ie repeating groups) and is thus the basic restriction which gives the flat file or tabular view. Moreover the formal definition of a relation as a set (in the mathmatical sense) of tuples (rows, records) ensures that every tuple is distinct.

Further normal forms assume this first normal condition to be met, although a similar theory of data can be developed without this restriction. Their objective is to prevent features of a relation which are regarded as undesirable and so should not be present in a "good" database design unless overriding performance considerations apply.

There are two basic ideas:-

- That some attributes act as "primary keys" for relations and serve to distinguish uniquely the particular tuple (row) instances.

- That there are dependencies among the attributes for a relation and particularly of non-primary key attributes on primary key attributes.

7.4.2. Primary Keys

The requirement that al tuples in a relation be distinct is usually met by the fact that one or more of the data items comprise an identifying key in a real world sense. It is, of course, business practice to introduce keys specifically to avoid ambiguity and for processing convenience. For example, whilst an employee's name will be used as the identifying attribute in a small organisation it is generally the practice to introduce employee numbers in a large organisation.

Given any relation it is possible to define formally a 'candidate key' as or more attributes in a relation which ensures uniqueness and 'the key' as an arbitrarily designated candidate key. Unfortunately this process, whilst being quite satisfactory when a real world key does in fact exist, can produce rather artificial keys for some relations for which there is no natural or obvious key.

Note that a restriction consequent upon the definition of a primary key is that its value (or the value of its components) can never be undefined. Primary keys are normally designated by underlining in the written form.

7.4.3. Functional Dependence

The basic idea is that a value of one attribute uniquely identifies that value of another attribute. Thus if we have a relation giving information about employees then a particular value of EMPLOYEE-NO will identify a unique value of SALARY (the salary of the employee corresponding to the value of employee- number), of DEPT (the department in which he/she works), and so on. This notion of a value of one or more attributes in a relation identifying the value of another attribute is, as we have explained it, exactly the same as the notion in mathematics of a single valued function, although our functions do of course change over time and our analysis is concerned with the database at any particular point in time.

7.4.4. Indirect on Composed Functional Dependencies

If we have two functional dependencies, say A -> B and B -> C then as a consequence we have A -> C. Consider for example :

EMPLOYEE-NO   —>   DEPT

(the department in which he/she works)

and

DEPT   —>   MANAGER

(the manager of that department)

then as a consequence

EMPLOYEE-NO   —>   MANAGER

(employee determines the name of the manager of the department in which he works)

Note that whilst the direct functional dependencies are determined as a matter of systems analysis the indirect functional dependencies are a matter of logical deduction.

7.4.5. Some Possible Undesirable Relations

Firstly consider the following relation :

Project -Request

PART-NO	PROJ-CODE	MANAGER	QTY-REQD	DATE-REQD
123	AAA	SMITH	60	4/7/88
234	AAA	SMITH	27	1/6/88
456	AAA	SMITH	100	9/9/88
123	BBB	JONES	60	1/9/88
-	-	-	-	-
-	-	-	-	-

We see that the name of the manager of the project will be repeated as many times as the number of different parts his project requires (or will not appear at all if the part requirements of a project have not been entered in the relation or have all been met - a tuple is deleted when the requirement is met). There seems to be unnecessary duplication of data because of the attribute MANAGER with consequent storage waste and unnecessary update activity and the danger of inconsistency when the manager of a project changes.

Secondly consider the following relation:

Employee				
EMP-NO	DATE-OF-BIRTH	SALARY	PROJ-CODE	EST-COMPLN-DATE
E012	1/5/50	10000	AAA	1/2/88
E234	9/7/45	12500	AAA	1/2/88
-	-	-	-	-
-	-	-	-	-

We see that the estimated completion date of the project on which the employee is working is repeated as many times as there are employees on the project, again apparently wasting storage and leading to unnecessary update activity and the danger of inconsistency when an estimated project completion date is revised.

Lastly consider the following relation:

Project-Resource		
PROJ-CODE	PART-NO	EMP-SKILL
AAA	123	DRIVER
AAA	234	DRIVER
AAA	345	DRIVER
AAA	123	MASON
AAA	234	MASON
AAA	345	MASON
BBB	123	BRICKLAYER
BBB	234	BRICKLAYER
-	-	-
-	-	-

There is duplication of data as the fact that the project requires a driver has been recorded three times because the project requires three different parts, each part requirement fact is recorded twice because two employee skills are required by the project. There is duplication of data and update becomes unnecessarily complex . Consider how we must proceed if a third skill is required for project AAA.

Note that in discussing this example we are adopting the conventional "closed world" interpretation of a relation, namely that not only are the facts represented by the tuples in a relation true but that all such relevant facts are presumed to be included in the relation (eg. the company's employee file contains data on all its employees and not just some). The "open world" interpretation is sometimes relevant - all facts in the relation are true but not all such facts are necessarily present - but is usually explicitly stated if adopted, otherwise the closed world interpretation is assumed.

7.4.6. Second Normal Form

We note that the functional dependencies in the first of the above examples are :

PART-NO,PROJECT-CODE	→	QTY-REQD
PART-NO,PROJECT-CODE	→	DATE-REQD
PROJECT-CODE	→	MANAGER

The unsatisfactory feature of this relation arises from the existence of the third functional dependency in which a non-key attribute is dependent on only part of the primary key. Hence the definition of second normal form has been formulated as:

A relation is in SECOND NORMAL FORM if each non-key attribute is functionally dependent on the whole of the primary key.

Note that a relation with a single attribute primary key is automatically in second normal form. To reduce the relation considered to second normal form we must eliminate the MANAGER attribute from it and ensure the information is stored elsewhere.

7.4.7. Third Normal Form

We can see that the functional dependencies in the second of the above examples are:

EMPLOYEE-NO	→	DATE-OF-BIRTH
EMPLOYEE-NO	→	SALARY
EMPLOYEE-NO	→	PROJECT-CODE
PROJECT-CODE	→	EST-COMPLN-DATE

hence

EMPLOYEE-NO	→	EST-COMPLN-DATE

In this case all non-key data items are functionally dependent on the primary key (and the relation is in second normal form) but EST-COMPLN-DATE only indirectly as a result of the composition of the previous two functional dependencies. We note that it is this indirect dependence which causes the duplication of data about estimated completion dates. Hence the following definition of third normal form which subsumes the above definition of second normal form:

A relation is in THIRD NORMAL FORM if all non-key attributes are directly functionally dependent on the whole of the primary key.

To reduce the relation considered to third normal form we must remove the attributes EST-COMPLN-DATE and ensure this information is held elsewhere.

7.4.8. Fourth Normal Form

The third example given above satisfies the definition of third normal form and yet is still plainly unsatisfactory. (It satisfies the definition because it is all key, no single attribute on any pair of attributes alone serving to identify uniquely the individual tuples). We note that there are no functional dependencies.

There are, however, two independent power set dependencies. By a power set dependency we mean that a value of one attribute identifies a set of values of another attribute. In this case PROJECT-CODE determines a set of values of PART-NO and independently it also determines a set of values of EMPLOYEE-SKILL. It can be seen immediately that in this situation and with the closed world interpretation we will necessarily have in the relation every possible pair of values of the two sets and the undesirable duplication will arise. We therefore make the following definition:

A relation is in FOURTH NORMAL FORM if it is in third normal form and does not contain two or more independent power set dependencies.

We see that our third example of an unsatisfactory relation does not satisfy this definition (it is in third normal form but not fourth). It must therefore be replaced by two separate relations, each of which contains one of the two power set dependencies concerned and both of which then satisfy the definition of fourth normal form.

7.5.   SUMMARY : THE STEP BY STEP NORMALISATION PROCESS

This process is useful if at the analysis phase we discover large complex records and require a systematic method to reduce such records to third normal form relations. It is this process from which the terminology 'first', 'second', etc derives. The process is :

- Remove repeating groups to give record types with a fixed number of data items (NORMALISE TO FIRST NORMAL FORM).

- Remove data items from records which are not functionally dependent on the whole key (NORMALISE TO SECOND NORMAL FORM).

- Remove transitive (or composed) dependencies and retain only functional dependencies within a record which are direct (NORMALISE TO THIRD NORMAL FORM).

- Ensure that no relation contains two or more independent power set dependencies and split any such relation into two or more derived relations to separate such dependencies (NORMALISE TO FOURTH NORMAL FORM).

The above process assumes that the dependencies among data items which the system is required to model are fully defined. In practice with large complex records this aspect is frequently the more difficult and once these functional relationships have been determined putting the data into fourth normal form is then a relatively straightforward matter.

FURTHER READING

- A Simple Guide to 5 Normal Forms in Relatiomnal Database Theory, W.Kent, ACM, vol 26, No 2, pp120-125, 1983.

- The Architectural Logic of Database Systems, E.J.Yannakoudakis, Springer-Verlag, 1988. (Chapters 6 and 7 give a review of normal forms).

8. CONCEPTUAL DATA MODELLING

8.1 INTRODUCTION

The conceptual model is the proposed mapping of the information gathered during the analysis of the existing information flow and structure into the database system. The definition of the conceptual model is the representation of the data in the database, independent of any database software. It is not constrained by the database management system in that it is intended to simulate the real world as it exists at the time and describes record content and relationships between records.

The Conceptual Data Model allows Data Analysts the ability to build a data structure :-

*   that represents the business view of data;

*   that is independent of performance considerations;

*   that can be used as the building block for a database.

Conceptual Data Model consists of the four following tasks: Entity Analysis, Data Analysis, Model Consolidation and Model Analysis. Each of these tasks involve a number of processes to produce certain deliverables, as shown in Figure 8.1.

TASK	ENTITY ANALYSIS	DATA ANALYSIS	MODEL CONSOLIDATION	MODEL ANALYSIS
PROCESSES	IDENTIFY SCOPE	IDENTIFY SCOPE	COMBINE USER VIEWS CDMS	VALIDATE SPECIFICATIONS & APPLICATION DESIGN AGAINST CDM
	DEFINE BUSINESS DATA ENTITIES	DEVELOP INTERVIEW PLAN	RESOLVE LOGICAL INCONSISTENCIES	ANALYSE & VALIDATE AGAINST PROPOSED BUSINESS PLANS
	DEVELOP BUSINESS DATA ENTITY DIAGRAM	COLLECT USER VIEWS		
		MODEL DATA PROCESSES		
		SPECIFY DATA ITEMS		
		CREATE USER VIEW CDMS		
DELIVERABLES	ENTITY DEFINITIONS	DATA ITEM DEFINITIONS	CONCEPTUAL DATA MODEL (CDM)	VALIDATED CDM
	DATA ENTITY DIAGRAM	USER VIEW CDMS		
	PARTICIPATION RULES			

Figure 8.1 : Conceptual Data Modeling Tasks

8.2   ENTITY ANALYSIS

A Data Entity is a person, place, thing, concept or event in a business that is of lasting interest to the organisation.It can be uniquely identified and have characteristics which are represented by data.

A list of Data Entities for any organisation can be developed from information obtained through interviews with management. For example, take the scenario of a fast food restaurant chain, called Fast Freddy's.

- Fast Freddy's owns 5 restaurants, one located in each of 5 towns. All 5 restaurants are identical.

- Each restaurant offers the same menu that features various products, including sandwiches, drinks and Fast Freddy's Famous Fries.

- The staff for each restaurant includes 3 types of employees: Manager, 3 chefs, and 4 food servers.

- Each sale is assigned a number which is unique only for that date and that restaurant.

- Each sale may consist of many products, each of which may contain several food items (eg. buns, mince, lettuce).

These statements would produce the following Data Entity List :-

> Company
> Restaurant
> Menu
> Product
> Employee
> Manager
> Chef
> Food Server
> Sale
> Food Item

For each Data entity, a definition must be written. The name and the definition should be stored in a Data Dictionary.

An elaboration of the Data Entity List is the Data Entity Diagram. This is the starting point for the next stage of Data Analysis. The lines, between Data Entities, show the relationships or associations between two Data Entities. These Associations specify the participation of the Data Entities and are based on business data rules.

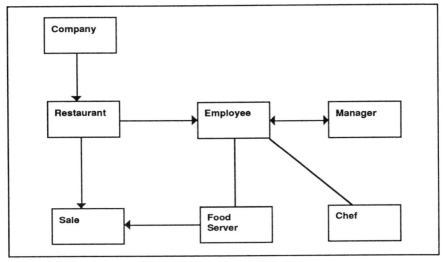

Figure 8.2 : Data Entity Diagram

There are 3 types of Associations :-

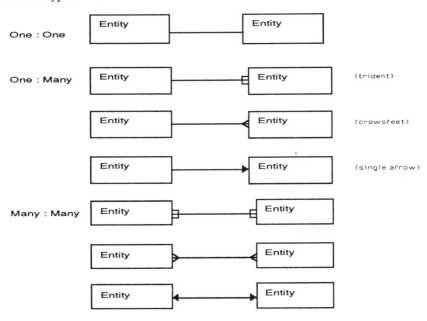

The Association Type can be determined in 2 ways :-

- Firstly, from the Business Data Rules. For instance -

a/   This insurance policy can cover many employees.

b/   An employee can have at most one insurance policy.

- Secondly, from the Data Entity meaning. For instance -

This restaurant employs many employees. An employee only works for 1 restaurant.

This is the restaurant that one employee manages. This employee manages only 1 restaurant.

Many to Many Associations have to be resolved by creating an intermediate Entity. For example :-

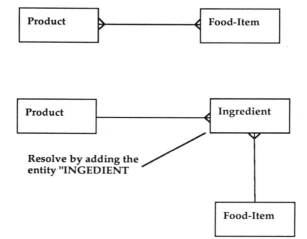

Outlined below are some guidelines for building a Data Entity Diagram :-

- Define the scope of the product

- Add only Data Entities of interest

- Use singular case

- Define Association Type

- Define Participation Rules

- Resolve Many to Many Associations

- Define any additional Data Entities

- Set a deadline for the project

8.3   DATA ANALYSIS

In this stage of Conceptual Data Modelling, we are creating normalised views of the data used in processes. These 'User Views' can come from any of the following sources :-

- Interviews

- Old Systems

- Old Files

- Prototype Panels

- Prototype Reports

The 'User Views' are identified during Functional Decomposition, in particular in the 4th Generation Environment through the prototyping of panels and reports (see section for more details).

When it comes to specify Data Items it is **vital** to have some Data Naming Standards, that are well documented, published and strictly enforced (1). The definition produced should facilitate the normalisation process.

The process of Data Analysis can be summarised as follows :-

- Preparation Phase

    * Specify Data Items

    * List the Data Items (record them in a Data Dictionary)

- Normalisation Phase

    * Define participation rules

    * Create Tables - these are the Data Entities and their associated Attributes

    * Add Data Entities

    * Select Identifiers -

An Identifier distinguishes one Data Entity occurrence from another. A Foreign Identifier where an Identifier is stored in another Table.

The guidelines for specifying Data Items are as follows :-

- Identify all Data Items in the Data Flow, or contained in the Prototyped Panels and Reports

- Use correct descriptive name from the Data Dictionary

- Verify the Data Item names and their meanings

The next stage of the process is to list the Data Items that are of interest to the project. The starting point for this is the Data Entity Diagram and the Data Dictionary.

The Participation Rules for the project have now to be defined. Only the Associations that are of interest should be included. It is important to remember that Associations reflect the business rules. At this stage, it is essential to define whether the Associations are required or optional, so as to ensure that the rules are clear.

Once you have the Data Items and the Data Entities, you can create the appropriate Tables. Then you can identify the Data Item or combination of Data items in each Table that will guarantee uniqueness.

Foreign Identifiers are used to associate tables. As all associations are either one-to-one or one-to-many, the procedure for identification is as follows :-

- One-to-Many Associations

    * Are the Data Item(s) of the Identifier of the Table with the single-headed arrow (or single line), also in the Identifier of the Table with the double-headed arrow, or crows-foot or trident ?

    * If not, add Data Item(s) as a Foreign Identifier in the Table at the Many end.

- One-to-One Associations

    * If the Identifiers from both Tables are from the same domain, do nothing.

    * If not, place the Identifier of the Table playing a role into the other Table as a Foreign Identifier.

Are you sure you have done everything ? It is important to remember the Data Analyst's Oath :-

"Each Data Items in a Table depends upon the Identifier,
the whole Identifier,
and nothing but the Identifier,
so help me Codd."

8.4   NORMALISATION CONSIDERATIONS

Normally, all that you hear about the Normalisation process is what I have talked about in the previous section and in Chapter n. However, the world is not perfect, and there are a number of inconsistencies that will need to be resolved. So what else should be considered?

8.4.1. Mis-Named Tables

For instance -

PRODUCTS (PRODUCT-NO + FOOD ITEM , PRODUCT-INGR-AMT, PRODUCT-INGR-UNT)

Does the Table "PRODUCTS" represent :-

- All Fast Freddy's products

OR

- Data about a particular product's ingredients ?

It is important to use the singular for the name of a Table and, in addition, it should reflect its meaning.

8.4.2. Mutually Exclusive Subtype Tables

For instance -

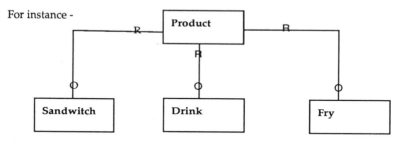

Guidelines :-

* can be at most one at a time

* Non-identifying Data items have meaning in the Table for a particular role.

8.4.3. Non-Mutually Exclusive Subtype Tables

For instance -

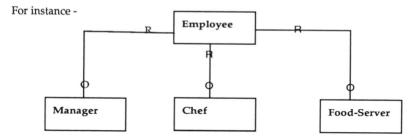

Guidelines :-

* can be some or all at a time

8.4.4. Identifiers

For instance -

RESTAURANT (RESTAURANT-NO , RESTAURANT-NAME)

Each of these Data Items will guarantee uniqueness of the other Data items in the Table.

8.4.5. Computer Generated Identifiers

For instance -

SALE (<u>RESTAURANT-NAME + SALE-DATE + SALE-NO</u>, ——)

These sort of Identifiers are needed if none of the existing Data items in the Table can guarantee uniqueness. They will normally have no explicit meaning to the end user. The application system will generate them and maintain them.

8.4.6. Derived Data Items

A truly derivable Data item value can be calculated at any time. However not all calculated data items are derivable. For instance -

EMPLOYEE (<u>EMPLOYEE-NO</u>, EMPLOYEE-AGE, EMPLOYEE-BIRTH-DATE, EM-PLOYEE-VACATION-BAL, ...)

Here "EMPLOYEE-AGE" is derivable if EMPLOYEE-BIRTH-DATE is known, and "EMPLOYEE-VACATION-BAL" is derivable if all the data needed for the calculation is available.

If derived data items are included on a Normalised View, then the derivable data item should denoted with a 'D'.

8.4.7. An Association between 2 Occurrences of the Same Table

There are 2 very obvious cases of this, namely Organisation charts and Bill of Material structures.

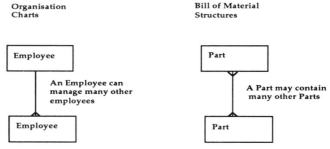

When this occurs, there always multiple roles involved.

In an Organisation Chart, we have the situation where an employee may manage other employees, and normally an employee is managed by only one employee. So we have a 1:many association between different occurences of the same table.

We have 2 roles being played by employees, namely that of managing employees and that of a managed employee.

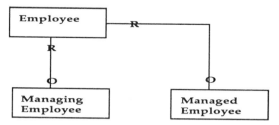

A managing employee may manage many employees. Whilst a managed employee can be managed by only one employee.

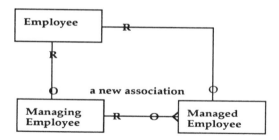

This would be physically represented by implementing as one physical Table as follows :-

Employee Table

EMPLOYEE-NO	EMPLOYEE-NAME	MANAGER-NO
115	Tom Clerk	125
117	Mike Smith	125
125	Mary Douglas	
310	John Black	125
500	Gary Frazer	310
510	Sarah Brown	310

In the Bill-of Material example, we can have the following scenario. A part can be made form many other parts. A part may be contained in many other parts. So we have a many:many association between different occurrences of the same table.

We must define the different roles that a part can play. The many:many association is really between 2 role tables - ASSEMBLY- PART and COMPONENT-PART.

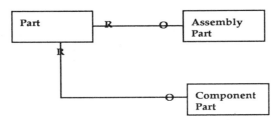

A part may play the role of either an assembly part or a component part. We must resolve the many:many association between ASSEMBLY-PART and COMPONENT-PART tables by including an associative table - PART-STRUCTURE.

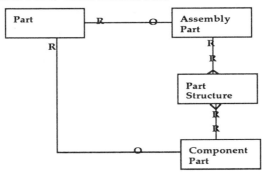

This would be physically implemented as 2 physical tables as follows :-

Part Table

PART-NO	PART-DESC
673	Engine
678	Carburator
742	Filter
812	Bolt
906	Valve
913	Pump

Part Structure Table

ASSEMBLY-NO	COMPONENT-NO
673	678
678	742
678	812
678	906
913	812

8.5   MODEL CONSOLIDATION

Model Consolidation provides a data model that is independent of physical design considerations or constraints, whilst stil containing all required data items and associations. The model is free of unnecessary data redundencies and has resolved all inconsistencies

The procedure involves defining 2 lists :-

*   Table/Data Item List, which lists all the tables and their associated data items

*   Table Association List, which lists all the 1:1 and 1:many associations between tables

These lists are populated from the Data Entity Diagram and the Normalised Views the inconsistencies between the two are resolved, so that a consolidated model is maintained to reflect the organisation's view of the data.

TABLE	TYPE	DATA ITEM
EMPLOYEE-WORK	U001	EMPLOYEE-NO
EMPLOYEE-WORK	N	RESTAURANT-NO
EMPLOYEE-WORK	N	SHIFT-NAME
EMPLOYEE-WORK	N	START-DATE
EMPLOYEE-WORK	N	WORK-HOURS
EMPLOYEE	U001	EMPLOYEE-NO
EMPLOYEE	U002	EMPLOYEE-NAME
EMPLOYEE	N	EMPLOYEE-ADDRESS
EMPLOYEE	N	EMPLOYEE-PHONE-NO
EMPLOYEE	F001	RESTAURANT-NO
FOOD-SERVER	U001	FOOD-SERVER-NO
FOOD-SERVER	N	FOOD-SERVER-NAME
FOOD-SERVER	F001	RESTAURANT-NAME
PRODUCT-SALE	U001+	RESTAURANT-NO
PRODUCT-SALE	U001+	SALE-DATE
PRODUCT-SALE	U001+	SALE-NO
PRODUCT-SALE	N	SALE-TOTAL
RESTAURANT	U001	RESTAURANT-NAME
RESTAURANT	U002	RESTAURANT-NO
RESTAURANT	N	RESTAURANT-NAME
RESTAURANT	N	RESTAURANT-PHONE-NO
SALE	U001+	RESTAURANT-NO
SALE	U001+	SALE-DATE
SALE	U001+	SALE-NO
SALE	N	SALE-AMOUNT
SALE	F001	FOOD-SERVER-NO
SHIFT	U001	SHIFT-NAME
SHIFT	N	SHIFT-FR-HOURS
SHIFT	N	SHIFT-TOTAL
SHIFT	N	SHIFT-TOTAL-HOURS

Figure 8.3 : Table/Data Item List

FROM TABLE	ASSOCIATION			TO TABLE
EMPLOYEE	R	1;1	0	CHEF
EMPLOYEE	R	1:M	0	EMPLOYEE-WORK
EMPLOYEE	R	1:1	0	FOOD-SERVER
EMPLOYEE	O	1:M	O	RESTAURANT
FOOD-ITEM	R	1:M	O	PRODUCT-SALE
FOOD-SERVER	R	1:M	O	REST-INVENTORY
FOOD-SERVER	R	1:M	O	SALE
FOOD-SERVER	O	1:M	R	SALE
PRODUCT	R	1:M	O	SALE-ITEM
RESTAURANT	R	1:M	O	EMPLOYEE
RESTAURANT	O	1:M	O	EMPLOYEE
RESTAURANT	R	1:M	O	FOOD-SERVER
RESTAURANT	R	1:M	R	FOOD-SERVER
RESTAURANT	R	1:M	O	PRODUCT-SALE
RESTAURANT	R	1:M	O	REST-INVENTORY
RESTAURANT	O	1:M	R	SALE
RESTAURANT	R	1:M	O	SALE
SALE	R	1:M	R	SALE-ITEM
SHIFT	R	1:M	O	FOOD-SERVER

Figure 8.4 : Table Association List

Guidelines for populating the lists are as follows :-

- Code data item types so that they sort with identifiers first and foreign identifiers last.

- Identify all data items or concatenation of data items that comprise the identifier of a table. Use a new group number if necessary.

- Do not attempt to correct the model at this stage

- Add a new line to the list even if inconsistencies occur

Once the lists have been populated, the inconsistencies within the consolidated model can be resolved. Data Administration must be involved in this resolution process.

8.5.1. Redundant Data Items

For these sort the Table/Data Item List by data item name, table name and data item type (descending).

Table Name	Data Item Type	Data Item Name
EMPLOYEE	N	START-DATE
EMPLOYEE-WORK	N	START-DATE

You have to ask the question "is this really the same field ?" .

8.5.2. Unnoticed Foreign Identifiers

For these sort the Table/Data Item List by data item name and data item type (descending).

Table Name	Data Item Type	Data Item Name
EMPLOYEE	U002	RESTAURANT-NO
EMPLOYEE-WORK	N	RESTAURANT-NO

In the example above the identifier in one table is used in another as a non-identifier.

8.5.3. Data Item Synonyms

This is where we have two or more data items with different names that mean the same. You must remove one form the model, if necessary renaming must take place.

8.5.4. Multiple Table Names

This is when you have two or more tables with the same identifier which are not sub-types. For example -

Table Name	Data Item Type	Data Item Name
PRODUCT-SALE	U0001+	RESTAURANT-NO
PRODUCT-SALE	U0001+	SALE-DATE
PRODUCT-SALE	U0001+	SALE-NO
SALE	U0001+	RESTAURANT-NO
SALE	U0001+	SALE-DATE
SALE	U0001+	SALE-NO

8.5.5. Association Errors

This is where different interpretations of the participation rules occurs. For instance -

FROM TABLE	R X:X R O O	TO TABLE
RESTAURANT	O 1:M O	EMPLOYEE
RESTAURANT	R 1:M O	EMPLOYEE

8.6.   MODEL ANALYSIS

Model Analysis involves the following activities :-

* Model Interpretation

* Model Validation

* Model Stabilization

8.6.1. Model Interpretation

The Conceptual Data Model is restated in business language in order that :-

* Table and Data item usage are consistent with the definition in the Data Dictionary

* All users have the same understanding of the content.

The model can be used to ensure that all the users needs are satisfied. This is done by posing questions at the model and seeing if they can be answered; the process is given the name of Model Interpretation. An Example of the sort of questions that could be asked are as follows :-

* WHAT IS THE MEANING OF THE TABLE "EMPLOYEE-WORK" ?

* DOES THIS TABLE CONTAIN THE INFORMATION ONLY FROM THE LAST SHIFT OF THE EMPLOYEE ?

* DOES THE DATA ITEM "NON-WORK-HOURS" IMPLY :

  YOU REPORTED TO WORK AND TOOK THIS MANY HOURS AS SICK LEAVE?

  OR

  THE HOURS YOU WERE NOT SCHEDULED TO WORK?

8.6.2. Model Validation

This process ensures that the global Conceptual Data Model supports all the CDMs which were combined to create it. It is used to validate the global Conceptual Data Model every time a new application design effort is initiated. Guidelines for the process are as follows:-

- Sequence the accesses to the data model to support required application services

- Ensure that all of the data items required are contained in the model

- Be careful not to omit derived data items

8.6.3. Model Stabilization

The model can be used to look at the cost of change. Here you are are looking at the cost of planned business changes now, compared to adding them later. The process is known as Model Analysis. An example of the sort of changes there could be are shown below :-

- DETERMINE THE LIKELIHOOD OF THE BUSINESS CHANGE

- DETERMINE THE COST OF MAINTAINING THE APPLICATIONS OF THE ORGANISATION THAT ARE USING THE DATABASES BUILT FROM THE CONCEPTUAL DATA MODEL

- DETERMINE THE NATURE OF THE BUSINESS CHANGE : EXPANSION OR STRUCTURAL CHANGE ?

8.7. SUMMARY

Conceptual Data Modeling provides the following benefits to an organisation :-

- Provides data/application independence.

- Presents data items in a clean and consistent manner.

- Minimises the impact of change to the database.

- Provides an orderly migration to integrated applications.

- Provides the foundation for good physical design.

FURTHER READING

- Pragmatic Data Analysis, R.Veryard, Blackwell Scientific Publication, 1984.

- Data Analysis for Information Systems, edited by R.Maddison, British Computer Society, 1978.

- Data Analysis Update, edited by G.J.Baker, DATABASE 82, British Computer Society Database Specialist Group, 1983.

- Data Analysis in Practice, edited by S.R.Holloway, DATABASE 85, British Computer Society Database Specialist Group, 1985.

- Database Analysis and Design, H.Robinson, Chartwell-Bratt, 1981.

9.   STRUCTURED METHODS

9.1.   INTRODUCTION

Before looking at the subject of structured methods, it is important to consider the meaning of the word "structure". Collins Dictionary defines "structure as :-

- Manner of building, constructing or organizing;

- Something built or constructed;

- The arrangement of all the parts of a whole;

- Something composed of interrelated parts.

The word "structured" is defined by Collins as :-

- To put something together according to a system.

The definitions above are all applicable in my view to the discussion of Structured Methods. It is important to see where these techniques have come from and what were the driving forces behind their development.

In the first decade of computers, the machines were very limited in their power and capabilities. This forced programmers to place a very high emphasis on the need to save microseconds and fully utilize core storage. The result of this was coding, which although efficient machine wise was frequently difficult to debug and maintain.

With the advent of more advanced computers the programmer is relieved of some of the problems associated with the older machines and can concentrate on the need to provide programs which are : easy to run, reliable to run, and straight forward to amend.

The phrases "structured programming", "structured analysis", and "structured design" are frequently used throughout the computer industry, but there appears to be no universally accepted definition of these terms. For instance, in the case of structured programming, it is often interpreted exclusively as a technique for improving the detailed program coding, whereas coding is really only one aspect of the concept of structured programming.

The honour of inventing structured programming and hence all other structured methods, is usually given to Bohm and Jacopini, who showed that all "proper" programs may be constructed from three basic elements, Sequence, Selection and Iteration, which were also constrained to one entry and one exit. The basis of this can be seen in the flowcharts of the three elements. In each case any process box can be replaced by any of the elementary structures.

In 1968, E.W.Dijkdtra published a letter entitled "GO TO statements considered harmful". In this letter, he argued that programming is a job for skilled professionals and that the greatest single factor affecting the readability of a program was "jumping" around, and that attempts should therefore be made to eliminate the "GO TO" statement.

These observations remained academic ones only for some time. It influenced the design of several programming languages, primarily ALGOL, but these also were in the main academic languages for the theorist only. IBM incorporated much of this early work in the design of PL/1, but completely ignored the principle of structured programming in order to produce a Jack-of-all-trades language. COBOL has taken to the present day to get official support for structure, and this is an addition to the existing language, rather than the required correction.

During the Seventies, further contributions were made to the subject by E.Yourdon with his book "Program Structure and Design". Yourdon also saw that the principles not only applied to programming but also to analysis and design. Here he worked with L.Constantine and published a book in 1975 entitled "Structured Design". Work in this later area of design and analysis was taken to its present state of the art by Gane and Sarson with their book entitled "Structured Analysis and Design". The techniques they advocated were and still are marketed under the banner of STRADIS.

In the UK, Michael Jackson was premier in the field of structured programming. He published a book entitled "Principles of Program Design"; this is the basis from which JSP - Jackson Structured Programming - was born. The company (MJSL) he founded, then followed the route taken by Gane and Sarson, and applied their techniques to design. In the early Eighties, MJSL launched JSD - Jackson Structured Design.

9.2. WHAT IS STRUCTURED PROGRAMMING ?

One thing it is not is just eliminating the "GOTO". You can write horribly unstructured programs that do not contain any "GOTO" instructions. There are those who would argue that you can write structured programs that include gotos, but they too are missing the point.

A properly structured program exhibits modularity, but not all modular programs are structured. Modules should represent more than conveniently sized sections of code, they should each perform a discrete function.

A structured language is also no guarantee of structured programs. This is especially true when the support for structured programming is added on to an existing language. Having an "ENDXXX" for every "XXX" is a not a complete formula for success.

Another supposed characteristic of structured languages is that they need no labels. Whilst this is strictly true, in that it is theoretically possible to write a structured program without using any labels, they are a practical necessity. Without labels, it is impossible to "perform" a common routine, and it would have to be inserted at every point it was needed. Obviously this is not an attractive proposition.

9.3.   WHY STRUCTURED DESIGN ?

Structured design is a prerequisite of structured programs. It is difficult to write structured code from a specification that says "go to Paragraph 13"! It is also desirable to analyse in a "top-down" manner to break any unit of development into tasks for individuals to perform. Accurate analysis eliminates the requirement for one programmer to wait for another's work to be completed, and thus saves time.

The process of systems design aims to develop a system which meets with the following criterea :-

- **Economic** - the chosen system should be cost effective compared with the alternatives which could be developed.

- **Accurate** - the outputs produced by the system must conform to the tolerences set by the user.

- **Timely** - the outputs must be provided by the time the user requires them allowing for re-runs if necessary. In addition, the system must be delivered to the user within a reasonable timeframe, that is agreeable to him/her.

- **Flexible** - business is often dynamic in nature and the requirements of a system could change over a period.

- **Robust** - the workload often changes seasonally, cyclically or perhaps even randomly.

- **Secure** - providing a regular service despite any failures of the hardware or software.

- **Recoverable** - if an error occurs it should be possible to recover from it.

- **Efficient** - not unnecessarily wasteful of scarce resources.

- **Reliable** - it should always work for known conditions.

- **Maintainable** - designed and coded in a way and documented so that enhancements can be made easily.

- **Implementable** - not unduly difficult to capture carried forward data at a moment in time to start off a sequence.

- **Compatible** - able to work with existing systems.

- **Portable** - not reliant on the facilities of one specific hardware configuration.

- **Acceptable** - to the design standards imposed by the organisation; to the users, operations, database administration and programmers.

9.4.   STRUCTURED DESIGN - TOP-DOWN

Where is the top? The first point to make is that we are not just talking about programs. We are talking about any unit of work; let us call it a process to avoid to much confusion. We can then put the label "program" on any process that fits the description.

The next point is that Top-Down design is an iterative or recursive process, so that the "top" will be redefined at each stage. It is in fact a requirement of the method that any process may be taken as the starting point for decomposition. Top-Down primarily defines the Direction.

Functional Decomposition is another name for Top-Down Design, and perhaps better describes what is going on. At each stage in the proceedings, we decompose the process we have reached into smaller units, until we can hand all lower levels over to someone else, ultimately the compiler for the selected language.

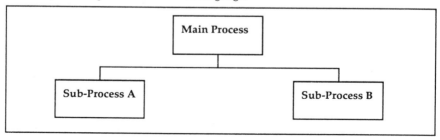

The work is quite straightforward, but there are a few basic rules to keep in mind in order to ensure a correct end result.

9.4.1. One Step at a Time

At each stage, only a single type of breakdown should be performed. There are three major types:

- **Sequence** - the main process is achieved by doing all the sub processes, in the order shown.

- **Selection** - the main process consists of a choice of sub processes.

- **Iteration** - the main process requires a sub-process to be repeatedly performed.

9.4.2. Completeness

The sub-processes must add up to the whole of the main process. Do not forget the error handling and just describe what happens if all goes smoothly. For certain proprietary languages, for example ADR/IDEAL, users will find that the editor helps by always providing WHEN NONE, ELSE and similar clauses to remind you.

9.4.3. Independence of Sub-Processes

When we break down a process, the sub-process should not overlap or interweave. For example this would be wrong

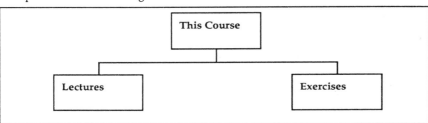

because the exercises are spread through the course. However,

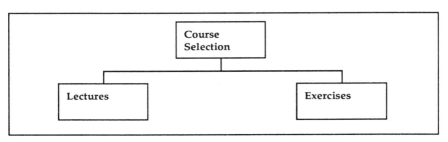

would be OK.

9.4.4. Dependence on Main Process

The sub-process must evolve entirely from the main process without any other considerations intruding. This is the hardest to get right.

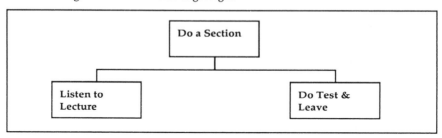

would be wrong because the leaving applies to the last section only.

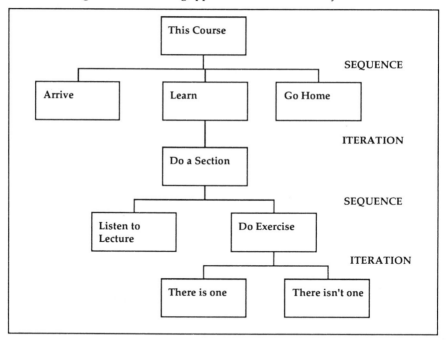

9.4.5. Notation

So far we have used simple boxes to represent processes, without any indication of their relationships beyond the downward direction of decomposition. Let us now introduce a notation to distinguish the types of decomposition. Leaving the sequence as before, we will show a selection by a small circle in the top right of the sub-process boxes. This may be thought of as representing the "tick the box" method of multiple choice forms. For iteration, we will use the asterisk, which many languages use as a multiplication operator. We will introduce further variations later as we refine the process.

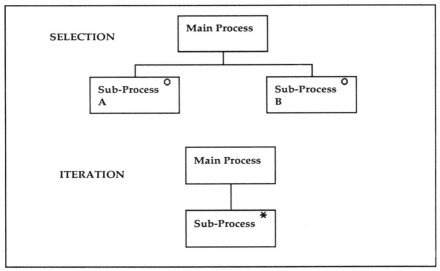

9.5. ADVANTAGES OF STRUCTURED PROGRAMMING

The advantages of structured programming techniques can be summarised as below :-

• Quantitative and Qualitative Benefits

• Maintenance

• Project Control

Quantitative and Qualitative Benefits have been observed in previous structured programming projects which highlight that , not only is it possible for programmers to write more statements over a given period of time, but, more significantly that the number of bugs in the program have been reduced.

In addition to the Maintenance associated with the removal of bugs which should have been discovered during testing, we are often faced with maintenance due to changes in software and user requirements. A survey conducted by EDP Analyzer suggested that the average organisation spends 50% of its budget maintaining existing systems. Experience has indicated a substantial qualitative improvement in maintenance once structured techniques have been adopted. As structured programs tend to be more readable and understandable, improvements and changes should be made more easily and less expensively.

While structured programming projects may not be finished substantially ahead of schedule they do tend to be finished on schedule. With top-down design, major program interfaces are established at an early stage thus eliminating potentially catastrophic bugs. The prototyping approach also often allows significant user orientated inadequacies to be detected at an early date. In addition it has been observed that machine time requirements for testing remain relatively constant for the duration of the project instead of increasing as the deadline approaches. Control of the project is much easier as there tends to be frequent target dates and so project members work consistently hard. Systems testing does not require the large amount of effort which it did frequently in the past; this further helped by the prototyping approach being used as well.

9.6.   FROM DESIGN INTO CODING

9.6.1. Constructs

Structured designs are easier to implement in a structured language. A major part of some books are concerned with the the conflict between design and implementation language but we shall avoid this by confining ourselves to properly structured languages.

A structured language provides framework elements called "constructs" that obey one simple rule. There is only one way in and there is only one way out. There may be more than one path through the construct, but all roads lead to the same exit point. For example, consider the IF construct:

```
IF condition
process-1
ELSE
process-2
ENDIF
```

Here it is clear that whichever process is performed, the next process is the one following the ENDIF.

It will readily be seen that the IF corresponds to a design Selection, except that it is restricted to a two-way decision. To cope with the more general many-way selection, there should be a form like

```
SELECT FIRST ACTION
WHEN condition-1
process-1
WHEN condition-2
process-2
WHEN ...

...
WHEN OTHER
process-n
ENDSELECT
```

The result of this is that we have a multi-way exclusive selection (only one process is performed). Should we want a many-way selection but non-exclusive, i.e. allowing more than one sub-process then we can use the following ;-

```
SELECT EVERY ACTION
WHEN ...

...
WHEN ANY
process-a
WHEN NONE
process-b
WHEN ALL
process-c
ENDSELECT
```

The presence of the summary conditions in the postscript of this form makes validations very easy to code. For example

```
SELECT EVERY ACTION
WHEN field1 is in error
DO field1-error
WHEN field2 is in error
DO field2-error
WHEN ...

. . .
WHEN ANY
DO reject-record
WHEN NONE
DO accept-record
ENDSELECT
```

This form of selection is not a pure structure, but rather a shorthand notation for a sequence of independent selections, each of which sets or amends the control variable that is tested by the postscript WHEN clauses. It would of course be equally valid to code it this way, but the SELECT EVERY method has the advantage of preventing corruption of that control variable by any other part of the code. It simply does not exist as far as the rest of the program is concerned. Beware however of allowing the processing in one WHEN clause to affect the conditions being tested in prior WHEN clauses. This destroys the legibility of the program, apart from any problems of reliability.

A notation to distinguish this form of selection in the design phase would be to fill in the circles for the exclusive form.

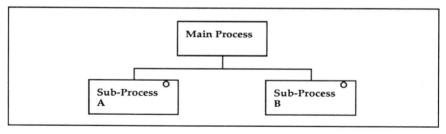

9.6.2. Iteration

In the design we have not indicated so far how we determine when to stop the iteration process. In most cases the iteration will further decompose into a sequence, and it will be possible to determine a point in that sequence where we can test for the termination of the iteration. A line can be drawn to mark this point and the condition annotated to it. If we make it a rule to always decompose the iteration, if only into a sequence of 1 process(!) we can add that line in all cases.

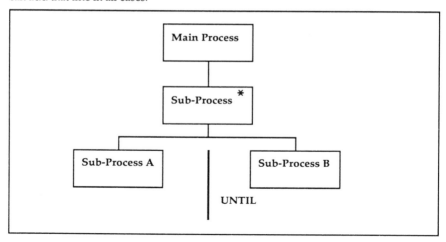

This translates easily into code as:

```
LOOP
Process1
UNTIL...
Process2
ENDLOOP
```

For example,

```
LOOP
GET transaction-file
UNTIL end-of-file
DO Process-transaction
ENDLOOP
```

Here we can only get an end-of-file condition after attempting to get a record, so the first part of the loop must be executed at least once. The process-transaction procedure will never be invoked if the file is empty.

If there is only one process in the loop, or we want a selection or further iteration next, then it would look something like this:

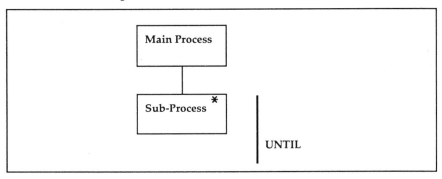

9.6.3. Other Constructs

In general, the constructs we have used so far are sufficient to write any program. However, in the case of many Fourth Generation Languages, other constructs are provided that combine selections and loops into more powerful units for file and table access. The FOR...ENDFOR constructs are a combination of a loop accessing the file with a success/ failure selection, even though some variants loop only once. The presence of combined constructs like these in the language should not alter the program design, but may require additional instructions to the coder to indicate how they should be implemented.

9.6.4. Resilient Coding

There are a number of simple things that will help to minimise the effort of maintenance that can be incorporated at the coding stage.

Use of multi-way selection rather than nests of IF's will make additional alternatives simple to add. A suggestion here is to test only FLAGs or other boolean-valued variables with IF and do everything else with SELECT. This also applies to multiple exclusion tests (If not

A and not B and...) Which are quite easily expressed as

```
SELECT
WHEN A
WHEN B
WHEN ...
WHEN OTHER
DO ...
ENDSELECT
```

If an IF is used, then always using a positive test, even if only the ELSE part is filled, will avoid recoding the test when both alternatives are needed.

A slightly more subtle form of condition testing is the UNTIL/WHILE terminating a LOOP. You might consider using a flag to indicate that loop processing is finished, which can be set from any process in the loop, rather than a complex condition in the UNTIL/WHILE itself. This means that adding a process into the loop, which may recognise another reason to stop, leaves the loop logic itself unaffected. Here we are decoupling the outer LOOP construct from the individual processes inside.

This sort of thing is not so easy when the loop is implicit, as in the FOR...ENDFOR construct, but here too we can avoid some potential pitfalls. If the number of iterations is known, then we should use a FOR FIRST n, rather than try to get out of a FOR EACH prematurely. If we are to stop at a particular record then specifying this in the WHERE clause is best. Isolation of conditions, i.e. avoiding the "1 means A is true, 2 means B is true, so 0 means neither and 3 means both", will allow sub- modules to be passed only one indicator - decoupling it from change to the other. To put it another way - bit flags are bad for you.

FURTHER READING

- Structured Systems Analysis : Tools and Techniques, C.P.Gane and T.Sarson, Prentice-Hall, 1982.

- Structured Analysis and System Specification, T. DeMarco, Yourdon Press, 1978.

- Principles of Program Design, M.A.Jackson, Academic Press, 1975.

- System Developmnent, M.A.Jackson, Prentice-Hall, 1983.

- Structured Systems Development, K.T.Orr, Yourdon Press, 1977.

- Structured Analysis, V.Weinberg, Yourdon Press, 1978.

- Techniques of Program Structure and Design, E.Yourdon, Prentice-Hall, 1975.

- Structured Design 2nd edition, E.Yourdon and C. Constantine, Prentice-Hall, 1979.

10. DESIGNING THE PHYSICAL DATABASE

10.1 INTRODUCTION

Once the Conceptual Data Model is complete, you will need to implement it into a physical database design structure. The physical design of the database is actually the mapping of the conceptual model onto the physical processing environment. The physical design is dependent upon the particular database management being used. Generally the process is at its most simple when the database management system to be used is relational. It must reflect the specifications for storage, access, etc. that are established by the database management system.

Since there will follow several phases of testing, several physical implementations of the database will probably be required. The first of these will only need to test the functionality of the developed system, and will normally use only small volumes of data. If the Database Management System has a truly relational data structure, then the physical database in this instance can be a simple implementation of the Logical data structure, with each normalised entity being represented by a table in the database, and with the prime key for each entity being represented by a physical key in the Database Management System's index system. Once the testing of application programs has begun. Statistics from the tools supplied with the Database Management System should give the information needed for first cut tuning of the physical database - depending on the capabilities of the Database Management System this will normally consist of specifying secondary keys to give access by alternative attributes, clustering several tables into a single physical dataset (or Area or Tablespace) to provide the maximum useable information per I/O event, adjusting block sizes and deciding on compression of certain tables for optimum storage, and ordering the physical storage of the data to optimize sequential processing.

The effect of these changes may be tried out on the initial test database before applying them to more critical systems, but some tuning will be sensitive to the volume of data or the rate of transactions, so tuning will always be an ongoing task of the Database Administrator. Again the selection of Database Management System will have an important part to play in the ease with which tuning changes may be made to a physical database design without having a disproportionate effect on the availability of the live database.

The characteristics of good physical design can be listed as below :-

- should accommodate future maintenance

- increase data availability

- satisfy the processing needs of the business

- allow data to be shared by many applications

- comprehend all integrity issues, covering both entity and referential through to business rules;

- provide for "optimal" performance;

- provide for data security;

- reduce hardware, software and staff resource requirements.

To ensure that you achieve all these characteristics you need the following information to do Physical Design :-

- **Data** - this gives you details about the Tables, integrity constraints and the Associations between Tables.

- **Process** - this gives you details about the type of access, the processing patterns and the Access keys required

- **Database Management System** - this gives you details about how you data model will be implemented by the software. Each database management system has its own particular characteristics that can be exploited.

- **Environmental** - this gives you details not only about the effect on your data of your hardware, operating system and TP monitor, but also to your particular business and political situation.

The goals of physical database design are as follows :-

- to implement data that supports the business requirements;

- to implement shared data models;

- to implement normalised data;

- to optimize performance by minimizing physical I/O's and maximizing logical I/O's;

- to exploit the special characteristics of your particular database management system.

10.2. MAPPING TO THE DATA-DRIVEN PHYSICAL MODEL

The Conceptual Data Model allows data analysts the ability to build a data model that represents the business view of data, whilst being independent of performance considerations, physical data characteristics and the particular database management system. It is therefore the starting point from which you build the Data-Driven Physical Model.

However, in addition, you need certain physical data information that is captured during systems analysis. The data information from both areas must be consolidated into the Table and Association list produced initially during Conceptual Data Modelling. This shown in Figure 10.1 and 10.2 .

TABLE	TABLE COUNT	DATA ITEM TYPE	DATA ITEM
ASG-TO-JOB-POS	0	U	ASG-TO-JOB-POS
ASG-TO-SHIFT	0	U	ASG-TO-SHIFT-NAME
CHEF	0	U	CHEF-NO
CUSTOMER-SALE	700000	U+	RESTAURANT-NO
		U+	SALE-NO
		U+	SALE-DATE
		F	FOOD-SERVER-NO
CUST-SALE-PROD	21000000	U+	RESTAURANT-NO
		U+	SALE-NO
		U+	SALE-DATE
		U+	PRODUCT-NO
		N	SALE-PROD-UNT-PRICE
EMPLOYEE	1200	U	EMPLOYEE-NO
		N	EMPLOYEE-NAME
		N	HEIGHT
		N	EMPLOYEE-BIRTH-DATE
		N	EMPLOYEE-PHONE-NO
		N	WEIGHT
		N	EMPLOYEE-ADDRESS-1
		N	EMPLOYEE-ADDRESS-2
		N	EMPLOYEE-ADDRESS-3
		N	EMPLOYEE-POSTCODE
		F	MAR-STATUS-CODE
		F	JOB-POS-CODE
EMPLOYEE-DEPENDENT	2500	U+	EMPLOYEE-NO
		U+	DEPENDENT-NO
		N	DEPENDENT-NAME
		N	DEPENDENT-BIRTH-DATE
EMPLOYEE-REST-WORK	4500	U+	EMPLOYEE-NO
		U+	RESTAURANT-NO
		U+	WORK-DATE
		N	EMPLOYEE-HRS-WORKED
		F	ASG-TO-SHIFT-NAME
		F	ASG-TO-JOB-POS

Figure 10.1 : Association List for Fast Freddy's

FROM TABLE	ASSOCIATION		AVG CARD	CARD VAR	TO TABLE
ASG-TO-JOB-POS	R 1:M	O	500	65	EMPLOYEE-REST-WORK
ASG-TO-SHIFT	R 1:M	O	1500	20	EMPLOYEE-REST-WORK
CHEF	R 1:M	0	1	2	PRODUCT
CUSTOMER-SALE	R 1:M	R	4	2	CUST-SALE-PROD
EMPLOYEE	R 1;1	0			CHEF
EMPLOYEE	R 1:M	0	1	1	EMPLOYEE-DEPENDENT
EMPLOYEE	R 1:M	O	4	2	EMPLOYEE-REST-WORK
EMPLOYEE	R 1:M	R	3	1	EMPLOYEE-SALARY
EMPLOYEE	R 1:1	0			FOOD-SERVER
EMPLOYEE	R 1:1	O			MANAGER
FOOD-ITEM	R 1:M	O	20	4	PRODUCT-FOOD-ITEM
FOOD-ITEM	R 1:M	O	60	10	REST-FOOD-ITEM
FOOD-SERVER	R 1:M	R	800	40	CUSTOMER-SALE
JOB-POSITION	R 1:1	O			ASG-TO-JOB-POS
JOB-POSITION	R 1:M	O	100	18	EMPLOYEE
JOB-POSITION	R 1:M	O	2	1	JOB-POSITION-RATE
MARRIAGE-STATUS	R 1:M	O	400	200	EMPLOYEE
PRODUCT	R 1:M	O	5000	627	CUST-SALE-PROD
PRODUCT	R 1:M	O	5	4	PROD-FOOD-ITEM
PRODUCT-TYPE	R 1:M	O	47	10	PRODUCT
RESTAURANT	R 1:M	R	20000	4000	CUSTOMER-SALE
RESTAURANT	R 1:M	O	50	6	EMPLOYEE-REST-WORK
RESTAURANT	R 1:M	R	28	4	REST-FOOD-ITEM
RESTAURANT	R 1:M	O	3	1	MANAGER
SHIFT	R 1:M	O			ASG-TO-SHIFT

Figure 10.2 : Table List for Fast Freddy's

10.2.1. Cardinality

Cardinality is a type of Integrity Constraint. For example :-

FROM TABLE	ASSOCIATION		AVG CARD	CARD VAR	TO TABLE
CUSTOMER-SALE	R 1:M	R	4	2	CUST-SALE-PROD

The first figure under the cardinality heading represents the "Average Cardinality". In our example , this means that there is an average of 4 occurrences of Customer Sale Product rows for every Customer Sale row. The second figure is the measure of the variability represented by a standard deviation; in our case this is 2. This latter figure is called the "Cardinal Variability".

The calculation for cardinality is a follows :-

- The population is all the Customer Sale/Customer Sale Product associations known

- Randomly sample 30 occurrences of this association

- Determine the number of products per sale

- From the sample size of 30 :

  * calculate the average

$$\bar{X} = \frac{\sum\limits_{i=1}^{n} X_i}{n}$$

  * calculate the standard deviation

$$\sigma = \left[\frac{\sum\limits_{i=1}^{n} (X_i - \bar{X})^2}{n} \right]^{\frac{1}{2}}$$

In our example, statistically speaking -

- the average sale will have 4 products

- 67% of the sales will have between 2 and 6 products

- 95% of the sales will have between 0 and 8 products

10.2.2. Mapping from the Conceptual Data Model

The data objects (Tables, Data Items, Identifiers and Foreign Identifiers) are mapped into the appropriate Database Management System format; thus producing a physical representation of data based upon only data information. For example, if your Database Management System was ADR/DATACOM/DB or IBM's DB2, Figure 10.3 shows the mapping.

CONCEPTUAL DATA MODEL		DATA-DRIVEN PHYSICAL MODEL
TABLE	maps to	ADR/DATACOM/DB Table DB2 Table
DATA ITEM	maps to	ADR/DATACOM/DB Field DB2 Column
IDENTIFIER	maps to	ADR/DATACOM/DB Master Key DB2 Primary Key
FOREIGN IDENTIFIER	maps to	ADR/DATACOM/DB Key DB2 Foreign Key

Figure 10.3 : Mapping for ADR/DATACOM/DB and IBM DB2

The Master Key in a Relational Database Management System must guarantee uniqueness to the other fields in this row of a particular table. The candidate key must be chosen that best represents the needs of the business.

10.2.3. Data Areas or Tablespaces

Data Areas define the groupings of tables; each grouping consists of one or more associated tables. The procedure for identifying Data Areas or Tablespaces is as follows :-

- **Identify Role Tables** - Role Tables are those tables that were introduced to name Associations. These tables contain the Identifier as their only data item. These tables are not included in the Data-Driven Physical Model. The Role Tables are indicated on the Table, as shown in Figure 10.4.

TABLE	TABLE COUNT	DATA ITEM TYPE	DATA ITEM
ASG-TO-JOB-POS	**0**	**U**	**ASG-TO-JOB-POS**
ASG-TO-SHIFT	**0**	**U**	**ASG-TO-SHIFT-NAME**
CHEF	**0**	**U**	**CHEF-NO**
CUSTOMER-SALE	700000	U+	RESTAURANT-NO
		U+	SALE-NO
		U+	SALE-DATE
		F	FOOD-SERVER-NO
CUST-SALE-PROD	21000000	U+	RESTAURANT-NO
		U+	SALE-NO
		U+	SALE-DATE
		U+	PRODUCT-NO
		N	SALE-PROD-UNT-PRICE
FOOD-SERVER	**0**	**U**	**EMPLOYEE-NO**
JOB-POISITION	10	U	JOB-POS-CODE
		N	JOB-POS-DESC
JOB-POSITION-RATE	45	U+	JOB-POS-CODE
		U+	JOB-POS-EFFECTIVE-DATE
		N	JOB-POS-RATE
MANAGER	400	U	EMPLOYEE-NO
		N	START-DATE
		N	COMMISION
		F	RESTAURANT-NO

Figure 10.4 : Table List showing Role Tables Identified for Fast Freddy's

- **Identify Small Tables** - These are Tables that have less than 100 rows. They represent DP tables used for Look-ups, Cross-Reference and Sequencing Numbers. These Small Tables are placed into a single Data Area and are identified on the Table List as shown in Figure 10.5 .

TABLE	TABLE COUNT	DATA ITEM TYPE	DATA ITEM
FOOD-ITEM	150	U N N N N	FOOD-ITEM-NAME FOOD-ITEM-SHELF-LIFE FOOD-ITEM-UNIT-COST FOOD-ITEM-STD-UNIT FOOD-ITEM-DESC
JOB-POISITION	**10**	**U** **N**	**JOB-POS-CODE** **JOB-POS-DESC**
JOB-POSITION-RATE	**45**	**U+** **U+** **N**	**JOB-POS-CODE** **JOB-POS-EFFECTIVE-DATE** **JOB-POS-RATE**
MANAGER	400	U N N F	MANGER-EMP-NO START-DATE COMMISION RESTAURANT-NO
MARRIAGE-STATUS	**5**	**U** **N**	**MAR-STATUS-CODE** **MAR-STATUS-DESC**
PRODUCT	400	U U N F F	PRODUCT-NO PRODUCT-DESC PRODUCT-STD-UNIT-PRC PRODUCT-TYPE-CODE CHEF-EMPLOYEE-NO
PRODUCT-FOOD-ITEM	2000	U+ U+ N	PRODUCT-NO FOOD-ITEM-NAME PROD-INGRED-AMOUNT
PRODUCT-TYPE	**8**	**U** **N**	**PRODUCT-TYPE-CODE** **PRODUCT-TYPE-DESC**
RESTAURANT	100	U U N N F	RESTAURANT-NO RESTAURANT-NAME RESTAURANT-ADDRESS RESTAURANT-PHONE MANAGER-EMP-NO
SHIFT	**3**	**U** **U** **N** **N**	**SHIFT-NAME** **SHIFT-CODE** **SHIFT-START-TIME** **SHIFT-END-TIME**

Figure 10.5 : Table List showing Small Tables Identified for Fast Freddy's

- **Place all other Tables into Data Areas** - All remaining Tables are placed into their own Data Area.

- **Group Tables that participate in a 1:1 Association** - The last step in Data Area definition is to identify all the Tables that participate in a 1:1 Association. These Tables are co-located into the same Data Area.

10.2.4. Database Desinition

The procedure for identifying Databases is as follows :-

- **Eliminate all Associations from the Association List that include Role and Small Tables.** Figure 10.6 shows this for Fast Freddy's.

FROM TABLE	ASSOCIATION			AVG CARD	CARD VAR	TO TABLE
ASG-TO-JOB-POS	R	1:M	O	500	65	EMPLOYEE-REST-WORK
ASG-TO-SHIFT	R	1:M	O	1500	20	EMPLOYEE-REST-WORK
CHEF	R	1:M	O	1	2	PRODUCT
CUSTOMER-SALE	R	1:M	R	4	2	CUST-SALE-PROD
EMPLOYEE	R	1:1	O			CHEF
EMPLOYEE	R	1:M	O	1	1	EMPLOYEE-DEPENDENT
EMPLOYEE	R	1:M	O	4	2	EMPLOYEE-REST-WORK
EMPLOYEE	R	1:M	R	3	1	EMPLOYEE-SALARY
EMPLOYEE	R	1:1	O			FOOD-SERVER
EMPLOYEE	R	1:1	O			MANAGER
FOOD-ITEM	R	1:M	O	20	4	PRODUCT-FOOD-ITEM
FOOD-ITEM	R	1:M	O	60	10	REST-FOOD-ITEM
FOOD-SERVER	R	1:M	R	800	40	CUSTOMER-SALE
JOB-POSITION	R	1:1	O			ASG-TO-JOB-POS
JOB-POSITION	R	1:M	O	100	18	EMPLOYEE
JOB-POSITION	R	1:M	O	2	1	JOB-POSITION-RATE
MARRIAGE-STATUS	R	1:M	O	400	200	EMPLOYEE
PRODUCT	R	1:M	O	5000	627	CUST-SALE-PROD
PRODUCT	R	1:M	O	5	4	PRODUCT-FOOD-ITEM
PRODUCT-TYPE	R	1:M	O	47	10	PRODUCT
RESTAURANT	R	1:M	R	20000	4000	CUSTOMER-SALE
RESTAURANT	R	1:M	O	50	6	EMPLOYEE-REST-WORK
RESTAURANT	R	1:M	R	28	4	REST-FOOD-ITEM
RESTAURANT	R	1:M	O	3	1	MANAGER
SHIFT	R	1:M	O			ASG-TO-SHIFT

Figure 10.6 : Association List Showing Associations Identified as Involving Role and Small Tables for Fast Freddy's

- **Identify Data Areas that are not named after "To Tables" in the Association List and build separate Database for them.** Figure 10.7 show this for Fast Freddy's.

FROM TABLE	ASSOCIATION			AVG CARD	CARD VAR	TO TABLE
RESTAURANT	R	1:M	R	20000	4000	CUSTOMER-SALE
CUSTOMER-SALE	R	1:M	R	4	2	CUST-SALE-PROD
PRODUCT	R	1:M	O	5000	627	CUST-SALE-PROD
EMPLOYEE	R	1:M	0	1	1	EMPLOYEE-DEPENDENT
EMPLOYEE	R	1:M	O	4	2	EMPLOYEE-REST-WORK
RESTAURANT	R	1:M	O	50	6	EMPLOYEE-REST-WORK
EMPLOYEE	R	1:M	R	3	1	EMPLOYEE-SALARY
EMPLOYEE	R	1:1	O			MANAGER
RESTAURANT	R	1:M	O	3	1	MANAGER
FOOD-ITEM	R	1:M	O	20	4	PRODUCT-FOOD-ITEM
PRODUCT	R	1:M	O	5	4	PRODUCT-FOOD-ITEM
FOOD-ITEM	R	1:M	O	60	10	REST-FOOD-ITEM
RESTAURANT	R	1:M	R	28	4	REST-FOOD-ITEM

Figure 10.7 : Association List Showing Data Areas Identified
as not being Named in "To Tables" Column for Fast Freddy's

- **Identify the remaining Data Areas and place them into a Database created in the previous step**. The placement is based upon the Associations with other Tables and the Cardinality of the Association (choose the Association with the strongest cardinality - average 1 - 30). Figure 10.8 shows this for Fast Freddy's.

FROM TABLE	ASSOCIATION			AVG CARD	CARD VAR	TO TABLE
RESTAURANT	R	1:M	R	20000	4000	CUSTOMER-SALE
CUSTOMER-SALE	R	1:M	R	4	2	CUST-SALE-PROD
PRODUCT	R	1:M	O	5000	627	CUST-SALE-PROD
MARRIAGE-STATUS	R	1:M	P	400	200	EMPLOYEE
EMPLOYEE	R	1:M	0	1	1	EMPLOYEE-DEPENDENT
EMPLOYEE	R	1:M	O	4	2	EMPLOYEE-REST-WORK
RESTAURANT	R	1:M	O	50	6	EMPLOYEE-REST-WORK
EMPLOYEE	R	1:M	R	3	1	EMPLOYEE-SALARY
EMPLOYEE	R	1:1	O			MANAGER
RESTAURANT	R	1:M	O	3	1	MANAGER
FOOD-ITEM	R	1:M	O	20	4	PRODUCT-FOOD-ITEM
PRODUCT	R	1:M	O	5	4	PRODUCT-FOOD-ITEM
FOOD-ITEM	R	1:M	O	60	10	REST-FOOD-ITEM
RESTAURANT	R	1:M	R	28	4	REST-FOOD-ITEM

Figure 10.8 : Association List after Third Step for Fast Freddy's

- **The Small Tables are put into a separate Database**. Figure 10.9 shows the result of this step for Fast Freddy's..

DATABASE	DATA AREA	TABLE
EMPLOYEE	EMPLOYEE	EMPLOYEE
		MANAGER
	EMPLOYEE-DEPENDENT	EMPLOYEE-DEPENDENT
	EMPLOYEE-REST-WORK	EMPLOYEE-REST-WORK
	EMPLOYEE-SALARY	EMPLOYEE-SALARY
FOOD-ITEM	FOOD-ITEM	FOOD-ITEM
PRODUCT	PRODUCT	PRODUCT
	PRODUCT-FOOD-ITEM	PRODUCT-FOOD-ITEM
RESTAURANT	RESTAURANT	RESTAUANT
	CUSTOMER-SALE	CUSTOMER-SALE
	CUST-SALE-PROD	CUST-SALE-PROD
	REST-FOOD-ITEM	REST-FOOD-ITEM
SMALL-TABLES	SMALL-TABLES	JOB-POSITION
		JOB-POS-RATE
		MARRAIGE-STATUS
		PRODUCT-TYPE
		SHIFT

Figure 10.9 : Data-Driven Physical Model after End of the Process for Fast Freddy's

10.2.5. Summary of Data Driven Physical Model Process

The Data-Driven Physical Model is where the Conceptual Data Model is mapped into the appropriate database management system format. For most data it is the recommended implementation. However, for data, where performance is more critical, the implementation must be more exact. Support for critical processes must be ensured by tuning the Data-Driven Physical Model based upon Process Knowledge.

10.3. MAPPING TO THE BUSINESS-DRIVEN PHYSICAL MODEL

Process specification needs to be data influenced, in order that the business requirements are understood, and the user needs are confirmed. It is important to know for each process what data is accessed by the process, th eselection criterea for the data and the sequence of the data on return. This is achieved through the concept of Access Maps.

10.3.1. Access Maps

An Access Map specifies the following :-

•   Type of access (inquiry, update, deletion, insertion);

•   Processing patterns (random, sequential, join);

- Criticality;

- Delivery constraints (response time, run time);

- Tables required;

- Access Keys required;

- Processing volumes;

- Frequency of the run;

- Location of the run;

- Fields required;

- Sequencing of rows;

- Access strategy (table joining sequencing).

Normally an Access Map is developed that looks like the example in Figure 10.10.

```
PROCESS : LIST WEEKLY SALES

        FREQUENCY :              50 Times per month
        LOCATION :               Local
        CRITICALITY :            4
        TURNAROUND TIME :        2 Hours
        PROCESSING PATTERN :     Join
        REQUEST VOLUME :         100,00

DATA REQUIREMENTS :-

RESTAURANT              (RESTAURANT-NAME, RESTAUARNT-NO,
                       EMPLOYEE-NO)
EMPLOYEE               (EMPLOYEE-NO, EMPLOYEE-NAME)
CUSTOMER-SALE          (RESTAUARANT-NO, SALES-NO, SALES-DATE,
                       SALES-TOTAL, FOOD-SERVER-EMP-NO)
```

Figure 10.10 : Access Map Example Part 1 for Fast Freddy's

But if you are to exploit the 4th Generation Environment, and maybe also to take advantage of CASE/IPSE tools, then you also need the SQL or Structured English constructs for the data accessed, and the the Associations between Tables that are to be used. Figure 10.11 shows for the example in the previous figure, this missing part.

```
PROCESS : LIST WEEKLY SALES

ACCESS STRATEGY :-

FOR THE FIRST RESTAURANT WHERE RESTAURANT-NAME = variable
       FOR THE FIRST EMPLOYEE WHERE EMPLOYEE-NO = MANAGER-NO
       ENDFOR
       FOR EACH CUSTOMER-SALE WHERE RESTAURANT-NO =
       RESTAURANT. RESTAURANT-NO
              FOR THE FIRST EMPLOYEE WHERE EMPLOYEE-NO =
              FOOD-SERVER-NO
              ENDFOR
       ENDFOR
ENDFOR

ASSOCIATIONS USED :-

RESTAURANT : MANAGER
RESTAURANT : CUSTOMER-SALE
EMPLOYEE : CUSTOMER-SALE
```

Figure 10.11 : Access Map Example Part 2 for Fast Freddy's

10.3.2. Processing Patterns

Processing Patterns reflect the usage of the data by a particular process. There are 5 basic patterns :-

- **Random Proceessing**
  For example -

Product Number	Product Description	Unit Price
1501	Hamburger	1.25
1670	French Fries	0.50
1803	Coca-Cola	0.75
1960	Vanilla shake	1.05

Process Task : Display information about a single product

Program Logic : Read a single row from the product table and display the informa-tion.

- **Sequential Processing**
  For example -

Product Number	Product Description	Unit Price
1501	Hamburger	1.25
1670	French Fries	0.50
1803	Coca-Cola	0.75
1960	Vanilla shake	1.05

  Process Task : Produce a product report showing all products in product sequence

  Program Logic : Read from the beginning to the end the entire table.

- **Partial Seqential Processing**
  For example -

  Customer Sale Table

Rest. Number	Sales Number	Sales Date
R1	A043	1/6/88
R1	A044	1/6/88

  Process Task : Report all sales for a given restaurant

  Program Logic : Randomly Read the Customer Sales Table. Then read sequentially until all sales have been processes for a single restaurant

- **Random Join Porcessing**

  For example -

  Customer Sale Table

Rest. Number	Sales Number	Sales Date
R1	A043	1/6/88
R1	A044	1/6/88

Customer Sale Product Table

Sales Number	Product Number	Product Description	Unit Price
A043	1501	Hamburger	1.25
A043	1670	French Fries	0.50
A043	1803	Coca-Cola	0.75
A043	1960	Vanilla shake	1.05

Process Task : Display a customer sale and all products in that sale

Program Logic : Randomly read Customer Sale Table Randomly read Customer Sale Product Table Then read sequentially until all products have been processed for that sale

- **Sequential Join Processing**
  For example -

  Customer Sale Table

Rest. Number	Sales Number	Sales Date
R1	A043	1/6/88
R1	A044	1/6/88

Customer Sale Product Table

Sales Number	Product Number	Product Description	Unit Price
A043	1501	Hamburger	1.25
A043	1670	French Fries	0.50
A043	1803	Coca-Cola	0.75
A043	1960	Vanilla shake	1.05

Process Task : Display all customer sales and all products in each sale

Program Logic : Sequentially read Customer Sale Table and randomly read Customer Sale Product Table.Then read sequentially until all products have been processed for that sale

The Processing Patterns have implications on the physical database design process as follows :-

- Random processes influence the selection of Access keys.

- Sequential Processes influence the selection of Physical Sequencing Key ('Native' Key), Single Tabled Areas and the choice of Shared Key-Ids.

- Join Processes influence the selection of 'Native' Keys (physical storage key), Access Keys, Multi-Tabled Areas and the choice of Shared Key-Ids.

10.3.3. Process Influences

To minimise the amount of manual work, only the critical business processes are included in the analysis.

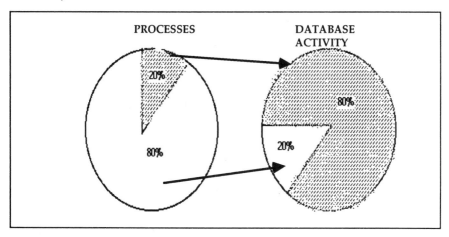

Figure 10.12 : 80:20 Rule

20% of the Processes of any System wil provide 80% of the Database activity. This 20% will be utilised to influence the Data=driven Physical Model. The critical processes can be selected from the Process List or from information stored on a Data Dictionary, in conjunction with the Access Maps. The selection is based upon :-

- Response time requirements

- Run time windows

- Business dependencies

- Processing dependencies

- Number of Database requests

A subjective ranking system based on a scale from 1 to 9 is a good approach.

10.3.4. Determine Utilisation of Keys

During the Data-Driven Physical Model derivation, keys were specified that uniquely identified a row within a Table, and that associate a row with another row. Using the Access Maps from the critical processes, you are able to specify additional keys required for accessability, and also the keys from physical sequencing on the storage medium.

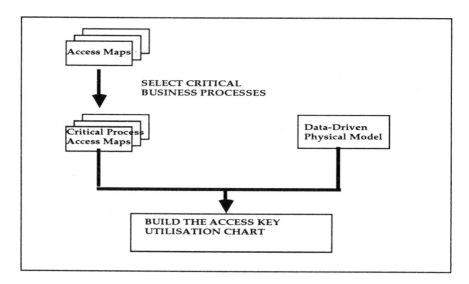

Figure 10.13 : Determining the Utilisation of Keys

An Access Key Utilisation Chart maps the Process Patterns onto the Data-Driven Physical Model, and thus details the usage of keys. In addition, the way in which Tables are sequentilly processed is highlighted. The process for building an Access Key Utlisation Chart is as follows :-

•   Create a column for Random Accesses and another column for Sequential Accesses;

•   Create a row for each Key defined in the Data Driven Model (Master Keys, Foreign Keys);

•   Group Keys together by Table;

•   Leave empty rows between Tables for the insertion of additional Access Keys.

The Access Map for each critical process is analysed as follows :-

• **For Random Processes :**
    * Determine Keys used for access;
    * Detail number of request in the random column for that key.
    Figure 10.14 shows an example for Fast Freddy's of these steps:-

---

PROCESS : INQUIRE EMPLOYEE WORK HOURS

        FREQUENCY :   30,000 per month
        LOCATION :   Local
        CRITICALITY :   8
        TURNAROUND TIME :   2 Seconds
        PROCESSING PATTERN :   Random
        REQUEST VOLUME :   1

DATA REQUIREMENTS :-

EMPLOYEE-REST-WORK   (EMPLOYEE-NO, RESTAUARNT-NO,
                           WORK-DATE, EMPLOYEE-HRS-WORK)

ACCESS STRATEGY :-

FOR EACH EMPLOYEE-REST-WORK WHERE EMPLOYEE-NO = variable AND
RESTAURANT-NO = variable AND
WORK-DATE = variable
ENDFOR

ASSOCIATIONS USED :-

NONE

Figure 10.14 : Random Access Map for Fast Freddy's

• **For Sequential Processes :**
    * Determine Key used for sequential access;
    * Detail number of requests in sequential column for that Key.
    Figure 10.15 shows an example for Fast Freddy's of these steps:-

```
PROCESS : EMPLOYEE LISTING

        FREQUENCY :                    30 per month
        LOCATION :                     Local
        CRITICALITY :                  8
        TURNAROUND TIME :              3 Hours
        PROCESSING PATTERN :           Sequential
        REQUEST VOLUME :               1,200

DATA REQUIREMENTS :-

EMPLOYEE                    (EMPLOYEE-NO, EMPLOYEE-NAME,
                            PHONE-NO, HEIGHT, WEIGHT)

ACCESS STRATEGY :-

FOR EACH EMPLOYEE ORDERED BY EMPLOYEE-NO
ENDFOR

ASSOCIATIONS USED :-

   NONE
```

Figure 10.15 : Sequential Acces Map for Fast Freddy's

- **For Random Join Processes :**
  * Determine key used fro intial request into the data model;
  * Detail the number of requests in random column for that key.
  Figure 10.16 shows an example for Fast Freddy's of these steps:-

```
PROCESS : EMPLOYEE-WORK INQUIRY

        FREQUENCY :                    15,000 per month
        LOCATION :                     Local
        CRITICALITY :                  9
        TURNAROUND TIME :              2 Seconds
        PROCESSING PATTERN :           Random Join
        REQUEST VOLUME :               5

DATA REQUIREMENTS :-

EMPLOYEE-REST-WORK          (EMPLOYEE-NO, EMPLOYEE-HRS-WORK)
EMPLOYEE                    (EMPLOYEE-NO, EMPLOYEE-NAME)

ACCESS STRATEGY :-

FOR EACH EMPLOYEE WHERE EMPLOYEE-NO = variable
    FOR EACH EMPLOYEE-REST-WORK WHERE EMPLOYEE-NO =
    EMPLOYEE.EMPLOYEE-NO
    ENDFOR
ENDFOR

ASSOCIATIONS USED :-

EMPLOYEE       R   1:M   O    4    2    EMPLOYEE-REST-WORK        60,000
```

Figure 10.16 : Random Join Access Map for Fast Freddy's

- **For Sequential Join Processes** :
    * Determine Key used for initial request into the data model
    * Detail number of requests in sequential column for that Key
  Figure 10.17 shows an example for Fast Freddy's of the steps:-

```
PROCESS : EMPLOYEE-WORK INQUIRY

        FREQUENCY :                    1 per month
        LOCATION :                     Local
        CRITICALITY :                  9
        TURNAROUND TIME :              2 Hours
        PROCESSING PATTERN :           Sequential Join
        REQUEST VOLUME :              3,500,000

DATA REQUIREMENTS :-

CUSTOMER-SALE                   (RESTAURANT-NO, SALES-NO, SALES-DATE,
                               SALES-TOTAL)
CUST-SALE-PROD                  (RESTAURANT-NO, SALES-NO, SALES-DATE,          PRODUCT-N0,
                               SALE-PROD-UNIT-PRICE)

ACCESS STRATEGY :-

FOR EACH CUSTOMER-SALE
        FOR EACH CUST-SALE-PROD WHERE
        RESTAURANT-NO  = CUSTOMER-SALE.RESTAURANT—NO
        SALES-NO  = CUSTOMER-SALE.SALES—NO
        SALES-DATE  = CUSTOMER-SALE.SALES-DATE
        ENDFOR
ENDFOR

ASSOCIATIONS USED :-

CUSTOMER-SALE   R   1:M   R     4     2   CUST-SALE-PROD              2,800,000
```

Figure 10.17 : Sequential Join Access Map for Fast Freddy's

For processes that use a key that is included in the Chart, but a different concatenation is required, perform the following :-

- Create a new row;

- Detail sequence of fields contained in the key.

For processes that use a key that is not included in the Chart, perform the following :-

- Create a new row;

- Detailed field(s) contained in the key.

Figure 10.18 shows the Access Key Utilisation Chart for the processes described in Figures 10.14 to 10.17.

TABLE/KEY	RANDOM	SEQUENTIAL
CUSTOMER-SALE		
RESTAURANT-NO,SALES-NO,SALES-DATE		700,000
FOOD-SERVER-NO		
CUST-SALE-PROD		
RESTAURANT-NO,SALES-NO,SALES-DATE,PROD-NO		
EMPLOYEE		
EMPLOYEE-NO	15,000	36,000
EMPLOYEE-NAME		200,000
MARRIAGE-STATUS		
JOB-POS-CODE		
EMPLOYEE-REST-WORK		
EMPLOYEE-NO,RESTAURANT-NO,WORK-DATE	30,000	
ASG-TO-SHIFT-NAME		
ASG-TO JOB-POS		
MANAGER		
MANAGER-NO		
RESTAURANT-NO		
RESTAURANT		
RESTAURANT-NO		
RESTAURANT-FOOD-ITEM		
RESTAURANT-NO,FOOD-ITEM-NAME		

Figure 10.18 : Access Key Utilisation Chart for Fast Freddy's

10.3.5. Determine the Utilisation of Associations

The Access Utilisation Chart maps the Process Patterns onto the Data-Driven Physical Model. The Chart details which tables are used together, and also highlights which tables should be considered for physical co-location within a data area. Only jJoin processes use associations, so only theses associations are used to build the Association Uutilisation Chart.

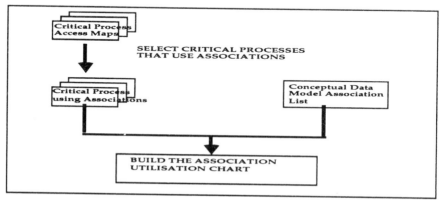

Figure 10.19 : Determining The Utilisation of Associations for Fast Freddy's

The process for building the Association Utilisation Chart is as follows :-

• Create a row for each association defined in the Conceptual Data Model Association List;

• Create a column to detail the number of times the two tables that participate in the association are joined together.

For each critical process that contains a Join Process Pattern analyse the Access Maps to determine the association utilised, and then place the number of joins into the Chart for each association utilised.   Figures 10.20 shows the Association Utilisation Chart based on looking at the example of Fast Freddy's previously shown in Figures 10.16 and 10.17.

FROM TABLE	TO TABLE	JOINS
JOB-POSITION	ASG-TO-JOB-POS	
SHIFT	ASG-TO-SHIFT	
EMPLOYEE	CHEF	
FOOD-SERVER	CUSTOMER-SALE	
RESTAURANT	CUSTOMER-SALE	
CUSTOMER-SALE	CUST-SALE-PROD	2,800,000
PRODUCT	CUST-SALE-PROD	
JOB-POSITION	EMPLOYEE	
MARRIAGE-STATUS	EMPLOYEE	
EMPLOYEE	EMPLYEE-DEPENDENT	
ASG-TO-JOB-POS	EMPLOYEE-REST-WORK	
ASG-TO SHIFT	EMPLOYEE-REST-WORK	
EMPLOYEE	EMPLOYEE-REST-WORK	60,000
RESTAURANT	EMPLOYEE-REST-WORK	
EMPLOYEE	EMPLOYEE-SALARY	
EMPLOYEE	FODD-SERVER	
JOB-POSITION	JOB-POSITION-RATE	
EMPLOYEE	MANAGER	
EMPLOYEE	MANAGER	
CHEF	PRODUCT	
PRODUCT-TYPE	PRODUCT	
FOOD-ITEM	PRODUCT-FOOD-ITEM	
PRODUCT	PRODUCT-FOOD-ITEM	
FOOD-ITEM	REST-FOOD-ITEM	
RESTAURANT	REST-FOOD-ITEM	

Figure 10.20 : The Association Utilisation Chart for Fast Freddy's

Information is mow available to :-

• Validate the Data-Driven Physical Model;

• Determine which tables should be co-located;

• Determine which Key-Ids should be shared;

- Group data areas into databases.

Remember not all relational database management systems will support all these functions.

10.3.6. Validation of the Data-Driven Physical Model

Each multi-tabled Area, except the Small Tables area, in the Data-Driven Physical Model is reviewed. The associations, which are implemented in the Area, are determined, and for each one table access analysis is performed to determine the join access and the sequential access.

The rules for Table Access Analysis are as follows :-

- When the sum of the sequential access by the 'native' key(the physical storage key) is greater than the join access seperate the data areas (tablespace) and move sub-type table into a new data area;

- When the association access is greater than the sum of the sequential access, then leave the two tables in the same data area.

10.3.7. Creating Business Data Areas

The procedure for creating Business Data Areas is as follows :-

- Identify critical associations;

- For each critical association perform the table access analysis;

- Based upon the results of the analysis either leave the tables in separate data areas, or combine tables into a single data area.

How do you identify which are the critical accociations ? Well, you use the same 80:20 Rule that was used for selecting the critical processes. To determine the number of critical associations, the number of associations are multiplied by 20%. The critical associaitons are those with the largest join activity.

Figure 10.21 shows the completed Association Utilisation Chart for Fast Freddy's, with the critical associations highlighted.

FROM TABLE	TO TABLE	JOINS
JOB-POSITION	ASG-TO-JOB-POS	4,000
SHIFT	ASG-TO-SHIFT	4,000
EMPLOYEE	CHEF	500
FOOD-SERVER	CUSTOMER-SALE	650
RESTAURANT	CUSTOMER-SALE	300,000
CUSTOMER-SALE	**CUST-SALE-PROD**	**3,000,000**
PRODUCT	**CUST-SALE-PROD**	**2,000,000**
JOB-POSITION	EMPLOYEE	300,000
MARRIAGE-STATUS	EMPLOYEE	2,500
EMPLOYEE	EMPLYEE-DEPENDENT	2,700
ASG-TO-JOB-POS	EMPLOYEE-REST-WORK	1,000
ASG-TO SHIFT	EMPLOYEE-REST-WORK	350,000
EMPLOYEE	**EMPLOYEE-REST-WORK**	**1,500,000**
RESTAURANT	**EMPLOYEE-REST-WORK**	**1,000,000**
EMPLOYEE	EMPLOYEE-SALARY	1,600
EMPLOYEE	FODD-SERVER	11,000
JOB-POSITION	JOB-POSITION-RATE	4,000
EMPLOYEE	MANAGER	1,750
EMPLOYEE	MANAGER	1,200
CHEF	PRODUCT	250
PRODUCT-TYPE	PRODUCT	54,000
FOOD-ITEM	PRODUCT-FOOD-ITEM	4,500
PRODUCT	PRODUCT-FOOD-ITEM	100,000
FOOD-ITEM	**REST-FOOD-ITEM**	**500,000**
RESTAURANT	REST-FOOD-ITEM	250,000

Figure 10.21 : The Critical Associations for Fast Freddy's

Figures 10.22 to 10.26 show the process for creating Business Data Areas based on the five critical associations in Fast Freddy's.

```
ASSOCIATION UTILISATION CHART :-
FROM TABLE          TO TABLE            JOINS
CUSTOMER-SALE       CUST-SALE-PROD      3,000,000

ACCESS KEY UTILISATION CHART :-
TABLE/KEY                                      RANDOM    SEQUENTIAL
CUSTOMER-SALE
    RESTAURANT-NO,SALES-NO,SALES-DATE          25,000    900,000
    SALES-NO, SALES-DATE                       114,000   15,000
    FOOD-SERVER-NO
CUST-SALE-PROD
    RESTAURANT-NO,SALES-NO,SALES-DATE,PROD-NO  14,000    20,000
    PRODUCT-NO, SALES-DATE                     0         450,000

TABLE ACCESS ANALYSIS :-
    JOINS = 3,000,000
    SEQUENTIAL = 900,000 +  450,000 = 1,350,000
```

Figure 10.22 : Critical Association 1 for Fast Freddy's

In the case of the first critical association, the best placement would be to place CUSTOMER-SALE and CUST-SALE-PROD tables in same data area.

```
ASSOCIATION UTILISATION CHART :-
FROM TABLE              TO TABLE                                      JOINS
PRODUCT                 CUST-SALE-PROD                                2,000,000

ACCESS KEY UTILISATION CHART :-
TABLE/KEY                                              RANDOM    SEQUENTIAL
CUST-SALE-PROD
     RESTAURANT-NO,SALES-NO,SALES-DATE,PROD-NO    14,000     20,000
     PRODUCT-NO, SALES-DATE                        0         450,000
PRODUCT
     PRODUCT-NO                                    900,000   150,000
     PRODUCT-TYPE-CODE                             0         0
     CHEF-NO                                       0         0

TABLE ACCESS ANALYSIS :-
     JOINS =  2,000,000
     SEQUENTIAL = 450,000 +  150,000 = 650,000
```

Figure 10.23 : Critical Association 2 for Fast Freddy's

In the case of the second critical association, the best placement would be to put PRODUCT and CUST-SALE-PROD tables in same data area. However, CUST-SALE-PRODUCT can only be placed in one area, and from the previous critical association it has already been placed in the same area as CUSTOMER-SALE.

```
ASSOCIATION UTILISATION CHART :-
FROM TABLE              TO TABLE                                      JOINS
EMPLOYEE                EMPLOYEE-REST-WORK                            1,500,000

ACCESS KEY UTILISATION CHART :-
TABLE/KEY                                              RANDOM    SEQUENTIAL
EMPLOYEE
     EMPLOYEE-NO                                   200,000    135,000
     EMPLOYEE-NAME                                 10,000     500,000
     MARRIAGE-STATUS                               0          0
     JOB-POS-CODE                                  0          0
EMPLOYEE-REST-WORK
     EMPLOYEE-NO,RESTAURANT-NO,WORK-DATE           87,000     400,000
     RESTAURANT-NO,WORK-DATE                       13,000     75,000
     ASG-TO-SHIFT-NAME                             0          0
     ASG-TO JOB-POS                                0          0

TABLE ACCESS ANALYSIS :-
     JOINS = 1,500,000
     SEQUENTIAL = 500,000 +  400,000 = 900,000
```

Figure 10.24 : Critical Association 3 for Fast Freddy's

In the case of the third critical association, the best placement would be to place EMPLOYEE and EMPLOYEE-REST-WORK tables in same data area.

```
ASSOCIATION UTILISATION CHART :-
FROM TABLE            TO TABLE                          JOINS
RESTAURANT           EMPLOYEE-REST-WORK                 1,000,000

ACCESS KEY UTILISATION CHART :-
TABLE/KEY                                      RANDOM   SEQUENTIAL
EMPLOYEE-REST-WORK
    EMPLOYEE-NO,RESTAURANT-NO,WORK-DATE        87,000     400,000
    RESTAURANT-NO,WORK-DATE                    13,000      75,000
    ASG-TO-SHIFT-NAME                               0           0
    ASG-TO JOB-POS                                  0           0
RESTAURANT
    RESTAURANT-NO                              25,000         200
    MANAGER-NO                                      0           0

TABLE ACCESS ANALYSIS :-
    JOINS = 1,000,000
    SEQUENTIAL = 400,000 +  200 = 400,200
```

Figure 10.25 : Critical Association 4 for Fast Freddy's

In the case of the fourth critical association, the best placement would be to put RESTAU-
RANT and EMPLOYEE-REST-WORK tables in same data area. However, EMPLOYEE-
REST-WORK can only be placed in one area, and from the previous critical association it
has already been placed in the same area as EMPLOYEE.

```
ASSOCIATION UTILISATION CHART :-
FROM TABLE            TO TABLE                          JOINS
FOOD-ITEM            REST-FOOD-ITEM                     500,000

ACCESS KEY UTILISATION CHART :-
TABLE/KEY                                      RANDOM   SEQUENTIAL
FOOD-ITEM
    FOOD-ITEM-NAME                              4,000      20,000
RESTAURANT-FOOD-ITEM
    RESTAURANT-NO,FOOD-ITEM-NAME               2,700     800,000
    FOOD-ITEM-NAME,RESTAURANT-NO              32,000       1,500

TABLE ACCESS ANALYSIS :-
    JOINS = 500,000
    SEQUENTIAL = 20,000 +  800,000 = 820,000
```

Figure10.26 : Critical Association 5 for Fast Freddy's

In the case of the fifth critical association, the best placement would be to leave FOOD-ITEM
and REST-FOOD-ITEM Tables in separate Data Areas.

10.3.8. Creating Business Databases

The business data areas developed in the previous step are now grouped into databases. These should contain tables that are frequently joined. The amount of join process activity is therefore analysed.

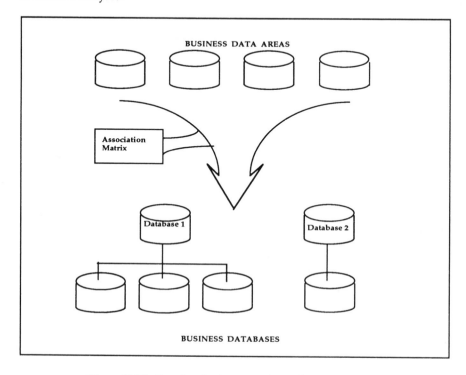

Figure 10.27 : Creating Business Databases for Fast Freddy's

The procedure for creating Business Databases is as follows :-

• Identify the critical associations;

• For each association identified place both tables into the same database; the tables may be in separate business data areas.

If we use the critical assocaitions from Fast Freddy's that were identified in the previous section as examples, the results are as follows :-

```
ASSOCIATION UTILISATION CHART :-
FROM TABLE            TO TABLE                              JOINS
CUSTOMER-SALE         CUST-SALE-PROD                        3,000,000

FAST FREDDY'S DATABASES :-
DATABASE             DATA AREA                TABLES
DATABASE 1           CUSTOMER-SALE            CUSTOMER-SALE
                                              CUST-SALE-PROD
```

Figure 10.28 : Critical Association 1 for Fast Freddy's

In the case of the first critical association, the tables CUSTOMER-SALE and CUST-SALE-PROD have been placed in the same data area and this does not need to modified. The two tables should be placed in the same database.

```
ASSOCIATION UTILISATION CHART :-
FROM TABLE            TO TABLE                              JOINS
PRODUCT              CUST-SALE-PROD                         2,000,000

FAST FREDDY'S DATABASES :-
DATABASE             DATA AREA                TABLES
DATABASE 1           CUSTOMER-SALE            CUSTOMER-SALE
                                              CUST-SALE-PROD
                     PRODUCT                  PRODUCT
```

Figure 10.29 : Critical Association 2 for Fast Freddy's

In the case of the second critical association, the tables PRODUCT and CUST-SALE-PROD should be placed in the same database. CUST-SALE-PROD is already in DATABASE 1.

```
ASSOCIATION UTILISATION CHART :-
FROM TABLE            TO TABLE                              JOINS
EMPLOYEE             EMPLOYEE-REST-WORK                     1,500,000

FAST FREDDY'S DATABASES :-
DATABASE             DATA AREA                TABLES
DATABASE 1           CUSTOMER-SALE            CUSTOMER-SALE
                                              CUST-SALE-PROD
                     PRODUCT                  PRODUCT
DATABASE 2           EMPLOYEE                 EMPLOYEE
                                              EMPLOYEE-REST-WORK
```

Figure 10.30 : Critical Association 3 for Fast Freddy's

In the case of the third critical association, the tables EMPLOYEE and EMPLOYEE-REST-WORK should be placed in the same database. Since neither table is in DATABASE 1, they should be placed into a new database DATABASE 2.

```
ASSOCIATION UTILISATION CHART :-
FROM TABLE              TO TABLE                         JOINS
RESTAURANT             EMPLOYEE-REST-WORK               1,000,000

FAST FREDDY'S DATABASES :-
DATABASE               DATA AREA                TABLES
DATABASE 1             CUSTOMER-SALE            CUSTOMER-SALE
                                                CUST-SALE-PROD
                       PRODUCT                  PRODUCT
DATABASE 2             EMPLOYEE                 EMPLOYEE
                                                EMPLOYEE-REST-WORK
                       RESTAURANT               RESTAURANT
```

Figure 10.31 : Critical Association 4 for Fast Freddy's

In the case of the fourth critical association, the tables RESTAURANT and EMPLOYEE-REST-WORK should be placed in the same database. EMPLOYEE-REST-WORK is already in DATABASE 2, therefore RESTAURANT should be placed into that database.

```
ASSOCIATION UTILISATION CHART :-
FROM TABLE              TO TABLE                         JOINS
FOOD-ITEM              REST-FOOD-ITEM                   500,000

FAST FREDDY'S DATABASES :-
DATABASE               DATA AREA                TABLES
DATABASE 1             CUSTOMER-SALE            CUSTOMER-SALE
                                                CUST-SALE-PROD
                       PRODUCT                  PRODUCT
DATABASE 2             EMPLOYEE                 EMPLOYEE
                                                EMPLOYEE-REST-WORK
                       RESTAURANT               RESTAURANT
DATABASE 3             FOOD-ITEM                FOOD-ITEM
                       REST-FOOD-ITEM           REST-FOOD-ITEM
```

Figure 10.32 : Critical Association 5 for Fast Freddy's

In the case of the fifth critical association, the tables FOOD-ITEM and REST-FOOD-ITEM should be placed in the same database. Since neither table is in DATABASE 1 or DATABASE 2, they should be placed into a new database DATABASE 3.

Any remaining tables are allocated to a particular database, by evaluating the amount of join activity to other tables.

10.3.9 Summary

The Business-Driven Physical Model is a process influenced Data-Driven Model. It represents the most stable data model possible. For processes, where performance is not acceptable with the Business-Driven Physical Model, a compromise may be required.

10.4 COMPROMISING THE BUSINESS-DRIVEN PHYSICAL MODEL

Compromises to the Business-Driven Physical Model should only be made in the following circumstances :-

- If there are severe performance constraints;

- If there are significant ease of use difficulties;

- If there are extreme political pressures exerted;

- If there are unique environmental characteristics.

Compromises may be found during design, or systems testing, or even after implementation. It is highly desirable to find them as early as possible !

There are four main types of compromises to the conceptual implementation :-

- Table partitioning;

- Redundancy;

- Repeating Groups;

- Derived data.

10.4.1 Table Partioning

Table Partioning is the process of taking a single table from the Business-Driven Physical Model and splitting it into two or more tables. Horizontal Partioning is dictated by roles. All tables will have the same columns, and the total number of rows will remain constant. Vertical Partioning is dictated by subtypes. Each table will contain only a subset of the fields and so the number of rows will increase.

The rationale for table partioning could be any of the following :-

- Performance for a critical application;

- Very large tables;

- Differences in request activity;

- Differences in volatility;

- Differences in availability;

- Differences in content;

- Differences in type of content;

- Differences in security requirements.

Let us look at a particular example to give a better idea of the problem. The example is a fairly typical manufacturing problem. We have a Part Master table, which consists of 300,000 Assembly-Parts, 500,000 Component-Parts, and 100,000 Raw-Material entries. The Business Rules, that we have, are as follows :-

- A Part can be an Assembly and a Component Part at the same time;

- Processing work load is spread evenly over all Part occurrences;

- All Part rows have the same columns.

The solution to this problem is to leave as one table, for the following reasons :-

- A row participates in multiple rows;

- There is a uniform usage pattern;

- There is acceptable performance.

10.4.2 Redundant Data

This is when the same data is physically stored multiple times. This must be avoided if possible, however if it is unavoidable it must be properly planned. tightly controlled and well documented. The rationale for the inclusion of redundant data is as follows :-

- Performance for critical applications;

- Reduction of access complexities;

- Better stability, where there is more retrieval access than maintenance access;

- Political pressure;

- Requirement of migration strategy;

- Requirement for special processing.

Let us look at two examples to show how to decide whether to have redundant data or not.

In the first example, let us consider the situation of filling orders in a warehouse.with the following business rules. When filling an item on an order it is necessary to access the Item Table to determine the Item-On-Hand-Quantity. The solution here is not to redundantly implement the Item-On-Hand-Quantity in the Order-Item Table as well as the Item Table, because of the instability of this attribute.

In the second example, let us look at a Bill of Materials processing problem. If say, it is necessary to produce reports in explosion processing that include Assembly-Part, Component-part and Component-Part-Description, then it would be quite in order to redundatly implement the Component-Part-Description, for reasons both of performance and the stability of the attribute.

10.4.3 Repeating Groups

This is when the same data item(s) are repeated multiple times within a single row. This process is sometimes referred to as "De-normalisation". The rationale for the inclusion of repeating groups is as follows :-

* Performance for critical applications;

* There is an absolute, definable, fixed number of occurrences;

* The number of occurrences will absolutely, positively **NEVER** change in the future;

* The users of the data understand subscripting;

* An attribute in the repeating group will not be joined to another field in the same repeating group;

* The master key is larger than the fields it identifies.

Let us examine the following situations, and see whether or not to allow repeating groups.

In the first situation, we are dealing with a driver licensing system. A driver may or may not have any violations, and there is a critical application that wants both the driver data and the violation data. Here, it would not be appropriate to implement the violations as a repeating group in the Driver Table, because the number of violations may change for any driver and there are a small number of rows within the Violation Table.

In the next situation, we are dealing with a Stock Keeping Table and an Inventory Table for a clothing manufacturer. Quantity is the only attribute in the Inventory Table. There is a limited and definable number of Sizes. Both tables are extremely large. If we have a critical application that requires Quantity by Size for costing purposes, it would make sense to implement a repeating group in the Inventory table, for both performance reasons and due to the fixed number of occurrences.

10.4.4 Physical Implementation Modification

Here we are changing the physical characteristics of the Business-Driven Physical Model. The types of modification covered are :-

• Splitting a large multi-tabled area (tablespace);

• Splitting a large database.

The rationale behind these types of modification are as follows :-

• Smaller units for back-up and restore;

• Smaller units for recovery;

• Smaller units for maintenance.

If we look at Fast Freddy's, the Customer-Sale and Cust-Sale-Prod Tables co-exist in a multi-tabled area. On examining the number of rows and the row length, the data area size will be found to fill one and a half volumes of disk. The solution is to split the data area, so as to give smaller units for back-up, restore and recovery.

10.4.5 Summary

Compromises represent distortions of the logical or physical characteristics of the Business-Driven Physical Model. They should only be made, when there are extreme environmental influences, as they always represent some form of degradation to the implemented physical model.

10.5. CONCLUSIONS

The physical design process for databases involves more than just the mapping of the conceptual data model onto the supported dat model of the database management system. It envolves understanding the business processes and the way that they will access the tables and data areas. As well the designer must understand the databae management system well, as it may have performance features in it that can be exploited. Finally, it must be remembered that political consideration must also be bourn in mind in the physical design process.

FURTHER READING

• Developing Data Structured Databases, M.H.Brackett, Prentice-Hall, 1987.

- Database Design Update, edited by G.J.Baker and S.R.Holloway, DATABASE 84, British Computer Society Database Specialist Group, 1984.

11. STRUCTURED TESTING

11.1. INTRODUCTION

Testing a system often requires as much an effort as developing it but, because it is one of the final steps, is not usually given as much planning as the earlier phases. This is a mistake which is learnt at great cost by many project teams. Early planning can ensure smooth and easy testing. Adequate preparation needs to be made before testing begins, so that it can be performed efficiently.

Testing and acceptance procedures apply to new additions of systems software, databases, and application software. These should be tested and accepted at each installation to assure their proper functioning and reliability before they are initiated into the operating system.

The aim of testing is to prove that the developed system addresses the pre-defined business requirements and will perform reliably and efficiently when running live. Testing can be divided into a number of phases, as shown in Figure 11.1.

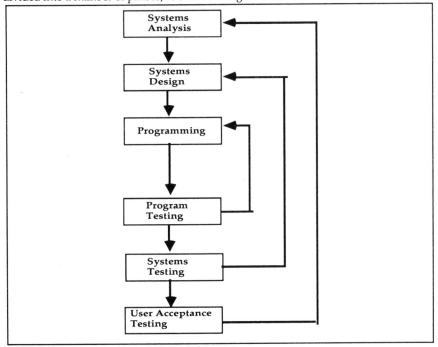

Figure 11.1 : Phases of Testing

Myers (1) defines testing as the process of executing modules, programs, procedures and systems "with the intention of finding errors". The emphasis is "on finding errors" and not simply ensuring the system's processes work when data is fed through them.

Structured testing can be viewed as the complementary process that ensures the outputs from Structured Analysis, Design and programming meet the user's specifications. The term Structured Testing is used because testing is directed at each level of structured output. In this context, the function of Structured testing has two objectives:-

- To organise tests using appropriate test cases which will provide the highest probability of detecting the most errors, taking account the economics and the time that can be devoted to testing in a particular working environment.

- To test each level of structured development in terms of the errors prevalent at that level.

Effective adherence to the second objective should reduce redundant testing.

11.2. PROGRAM TESTING

The purpose of program testing is to check that the program is working according to specification and that every path executes as expected. The objectives in designing a testing strategy are to ensure that the programmer's understanding of the function of the program is correct and that all parts of the program are thoroughly checked as efficiently as possible.

It is necessary to demonstrate that the program performs as specified. The amount of testing can range from testing just the main logic flow, through testing every branch once or every logical path once, to testing each logical module with all combinations of input. Normally every path of the program must be executed at least once and every major combination of conditions must be tested, including the error conditions. The detailed design of the testing strategy is one of the most crucial areas of programming and, if badly designed, is one of the most common causes of failure to meet system specifications and target dates. To ensure that the test strategy is well designed and comprehensive, a formalised approach should be used.

The simplest method of testing a program is to compile all logical modules and then test the whole program. There are three main alternatives to this approach, namely top-down, bottom-up and isolation and linkage testing. These all differ in the sequence in which the logical modules are coded and the techniques used to pass data to and from the components under test.

11.3. SYSTEMS TESTING

During Systems Testing the system is verified to operate correctly and according to design specifications even under stress conditions. It should also show that the system will interface correctly with other existing computer systems. The running of the system test should be under the control of operations, so that it can also prove that operating procedures are correct. There should be sufficient volume of data to demonstrate that the system meets performance constraints. System security and recovery procedures must be tested, as must all cyclic and periodic runs and all interface conditions between programs. The design of the system testing is an integral part of the system design, so it should be performed as a task during the design phase. User and operational documentation and training materials are also verified to be correct and complete. Final preparations are made for full user training and conversion to the new system.

The method of system test planning is related to structured system design. It utilises the documentation that has been built up during functional decomposition and the logical and physical design. From this documentation, the tests and runs which are required are specified. The data needed can be created with assistance from the users, and both the volume and content of the data can be controlled by use of cross-referencing techniques.

The Products of this phase are :-

* an operational system working according to design specifications

* completed and verified user and operational documentation

* specific security specifications

* user and operational training

* required hardware and software installed and available for use

* detailed plans for installation

11.4.   USER ACCEPTANCE TESTING

The degree of user acceptance testing to be performed must be established and agreed during analysis. It may be that the system will be run in parallel with the existing system or with part of the existing system, or that the users will create special test data. The key difference between system testing and user acceptance testing is that users are testing the system as a black box and are only interested in the inputs and outputs. As well as testing the computer system, the users must also test the clerical procedures. The decision on the plan for user acceptance testing lies with user management, which is responsible for staff levels and schedules. The details of the plan must be the responsibility of the analyst/ project leader who can establish the right environment within the constraints set.

11.5. TESTING STRATEGIES

Five basic testing strategies can be used to perform structured testing. These are:-

• Black Box Testing

• White Box Testing

• Inspections and Walkthroughs

• Incremental Testing

• Non-Incremental Testing

•. Top-Down and Bottom-Up Testing

11.5.1. Black Box Testing

In this strategy, the tester views the module, program, procedure, or system as a "black box" and is completely unconcerned about its internal behaviour and structure. The tester is only concerned with finding the circumstances in which the process does not behave according to its specifications. Test data are derived in terms of output related to input, and without reference to the internal logic of the process.

11.5.2. White Box Testing

This is the exact opposite of black box testing. In this strategy, the tester is concerned with the flow and structure of the internal logic of the process. Testing is intended to ensure that every executable statement, decision and condition is tested at least once.

11.5.3. Inspections and Walkthroughs

Inspections and Walkthroughs are the reading or visual inspection of a process in structured English, Pseudo Code or Code by a team of testers, with the sole objective of detecting errors, but not to find solutions to the errors detected. The latter is part of the design and development function and is not part of the testing function.

11.5.4. Incremental Testing

In Incremental testing, one process is combined with a previously tested set of processes until the whole hierarchy is tested. The use of this form of testing can be applied to the integration of modules or, at the other end of the spectrum to the integration of programs and sub-systems.

11.5.5. Non-Incremental Testing

This is the opposite of Incremental testing. Each process is tested independently and then combined in one or more major integration tests. This type of testing is sometimes referred to as "Big-Bang" testing, as that is quite often what happens to the system after the test is done! This occurs because the interfaces do not fit together.

11.5.6. Top-Down and Bottom-Up Testing

Top-Down and Bottom-Up testing apply particularly to module integration. With Top-Down testing, testing commences with the highest level module in the hierarchy and proceeds downwards. Bottom-Up testing commences with the modules at the bottom and integrates the modules at the next highest level till the top level is reached. A major advantage of top-Down testing over Bottom-Up testing is, that this strategy enables the tester to test the highest level modules for particular programs or sub-systems together before the lower levels are coded and tested, to ensure the inputs and outputs between programs or sub-systems interface properly and, as a result, the sub-system or system structure meets specification.

11.6.   TESTING TECHNIQUES

Several techniques can be used with the testing strategies describes in the previous section. Myers (1) describes these techniques in considerable detail.   Among the techniques described are those for the testing of statements, decisions and conditions found in the module or program logic while performing White box testing. Other techniques include "Equivalence Partitioning", "Boundary Value Analysis", "Cause-Effect Graphing" and "Error Guessing".

11.6.1. Equivalence Partitioning
This technique is used to divide all inputs or outputs into "equivalent" classes, ie any value tested within this class may be assumed to apply to all other values in the same "equivalent" class. For example, if a salary scale has the following ranges:

Range A	£10,000 - £12,000
Range B	£11,000 - £13,000
Range C	£12,000 - £14,000

then each range within the scale may be considered an "equivalence" class, and any value within a range should produce the same result as any other value within that range.

11.6.2. Boundary Value Analysis

This technique compliments "Equivalence Partitioning" as it implies using test data whose values fall outside the "Equivalence" class. In the salary scale example above, in Range B, a value of £10,999 or £13,001 will fall outside the range.

11.6.3. Cause Effect Graphing

This is a technique which involves the identification of all possible causes and effects in the process logic, the charting of the cause-effect combinations into a cause-effect graph and the conversion of this cause-effect graph into a decision table. The latter then provides test cases necessary to test the logic of the module or program. "Cause-Effect Graphing" does not lend itself to simple illustrations such as those used in describing "Equivalence Partitioning" or "Boundary Value Analysis".

11.6.4. Error Guessing

This is probably the oldest and commonest technique for generating test data and it is largely an intuitive process. The basic idea is to enumerate a list of possible errors or error prone situations and then develop test cases based on this list.

11.7. TEST PLANS

Each test plan is unique as it must only be designed to meet the objectives of the test level, but should take into account the different variables that effect the development or modification of the system being tested. The following items can serve as a check list for the different stages of the test plan.

11.7.1. Outline Test Plan

The major objective of this outline test plan is to identify, estimate and schedule both time and activities to be completed during testing. The plan is the responsibility of the project leader, but has to be formulated by consultation with users, operations and data administration. It is important to agree the amount of user participation and assign specific tasks to members of the user departments concerned.

The documentation produced will consist of: -

• A system test strategy statement

- A network to show overall dependencies

- A bar chart to show time scales and resources

- A brief narrative of the specific areas in each activity and a statement of assumptions.

The plan must be walked through by all parties who were consulted during its preparation. It is important that they all agree the estimates and commit themselves to the plan.

As well as producing an outline test plan, at this stage it is good idea to agree a formal procedure for handling errors, for review meetings on testing and for training user staff in the skills required. It may also be necessary to plan the conversion of existing computer and manual files and to detail any specific software the users will need to set up data.

11.7.2. Detailed Plan

Once the design of the system has been produced, the outline test plan can be refined and expanded. This will be the responsibility of the project leader, consulting other departments as for the outline test plan. The documentation produced will be a refined version of the outline test plan and a similar walkthrough is held.

In addition to scheduling that activities directly related to producing test data, it is necessary to consider if any software testing aids are required. Typical examples are data generators, file-compare utilities, file-print utilities and performance monitors. They may be supplied by a manufacturer, software house or written by the project team. If the latter, then that system design should be studied carefully to take advantage of any code which is to be generated as part of the system and is applicable to the testing aids.

11.7.3. Business Test Conditions

This activity consists of identifying test conditions which reflect the business view of the system as seen by the users. It is completed by the analysts with assistance from the users. The method of creating the checklists is to follow each input through its life and to list the conditions to be tested. All valid and invalid conditions must be checked. When all the inputs have been followed, the outputs should be examined to ascertain that all the conditions for each output will be tested. As a large number of checklists will be produced, reviews should be held periodically on a logically grouped set of lists.

11.7.4. Interface Test Conditions

This activity is performed by the system designers after system design has been produced It involves listing the conditions arising from the interface between the system to be tested and other existing systems. Checklists are produced by each interface file, and common database file. The same form is used as for listing business conditions. Walkthroughs should be held with the people responsible for the interfacing systems.

11.7.5 Technical Test Conditions

This activity entails the system designers listing all processing conditions to be tested in the system. During Functional decomposition, structure charts and/or data flow diagrams were produced defining the processing on one piece of data. These charts and/or diagrams are used to work out the transaction profiles and hence the programs needed. These charts and/or diagrams should also be used to assist in the specification of the process conditions which must be tested. A large number of checklists will be produced and so they should also be reviewed in logical groups, so that no review takes longer than one hour.

11.7.6. Test Condition Combinations

This activity will combine the different test conditions identified in the previous steps into test cases. Each test case will consist of one or more business conditions, technical conditions and interface conditions relating to a particular logical section of the system. These conditions must be combined to reflect the realistic operational situation where interaction between conditions may occur. Walkthroughs are performed on related sets of combinations.

11.7.7. Test Run Structuring

The system designers combine test cases into runs and produce a plan indicating the dependencies between runs. A run could be a batch runstream or it could equally be a set transactions to be used in a particular sequence to be used for an online test. Test cases should be cross-referenced to runs to ensure that all the test cases are incorporated.. In addition, the designers should also document the estimates of machine time and resources of people and terminals that will be needed. The plan must be reviewed and agreed by Operations.

11.7.8. Test Data Requirements

Once the test cases have been combined into runs, test data can be prepared. If possible, the users should participate in this task. A strategy must be adopted on the quickest method to obtain all the data required. It could be any or a combination of the following:-

- Generated by a test data generator;

- Set up by the project team;

- Set up by the users;

- Created by another computer system;

- Extracted from live computer files;

- Extracted from live manual files.

The aim is obtain the minimum amount of test data which will check all specific conditions. This usually means that the extraction from a live computer file will be insufficient, because it would be unlikely for all the conditions to occur. A combination of techniques can be used to overcome this problem.

11.7.9. Expected Results Preparation

Once the data has been created, the expected results can be predicted for each test condition. This is a long and laborious task but saves much time during the checking of test results. The overall result of a test should be documented together with the old and new values of the relevant fields. It may also be necessary to generate specimen reports. Control totals must be calculated and any console or terminal message expected noted.

11.7.10. Test JCL Preparation

The operational JCL can be produced during the final stages of development. This activity should be coordinated by operations support to ensure that the JCL will be suitable for live running. It is possible to create JCL procedures which are laid out clearly and well documented in much the same manner that program code is formulated. This should be done so that it is easy to understand the JCL, and recovery and restart can be achieved as simply as possible.

11.7.11. Test Scheduling

This activity involves estimating the number of test slots required for each test run specified. In addition, the existence of any dependence among test runs must be identified. When these stages have been completed, then the schedule can be devised, incorporating resources required, in conjunction with the operations. For each test run specified, the machine requirements must be detailed. These include tape/disk requirements, performance monitoring software, special stationary, etc. The schedule must be agreed with all the parties controlling the resources required and with the users if they are to participate in the checking of results.

11.7.12. Test Submission

This is the final task within the system testing phase. It involves submitting the test according to the schedule. It is best if operations control the submission and running of all batch tests, as this will ensure the operational procedures are complete. For online systems, operations support should fulfill their normal role as if the system was live. Once again this will ensure that the operational procedures are complete. It is suggested that for online testing, test scripts are used to indicate to the terminal operator the input required. The operator must enter the results on these scripts and return them to the project team for checking.

11.7.13. Test Checkout

The actual and expected results must be compared and all differences/errors identified. When a difference is determined to be an error in the system rather than in the expected results, a fault log is completed. This fault log describes the error and how it was found, giving precise details of the test run and data and any references to the files and outputs which are available. If the fault can immediately be assigned to a particular program or in the case of batch to a JCL procedure, it can be handed over for amendment. However, if there is the slightest doubt what caused the problem, action should be deferred until it has been carefully analysed.

11.7.14. Test Performance Review

Most systems will have been set performance constraints of some sort. For example, run times for batch systems and cpu utilisation and response times for online systems. Whatever the constraints, they must be checked during systems testing to demonstrate that they have been met. The easiest way to do this is to use a performance monitor and check its results against those predicted. Often test data volumes will need to be enhanced to simulate design volumes.

11.7.15. Test Problem Evaluation

After each testing session, the source of all errors identified must be discovered. The fault may be machine or operational error; it may have been caused by a mistake in the JCL procedure or by the test data files which were used; or it may be a program or system bug. The last two usually take the longest to correct and may require the test schedule to be amended. As the errors are corrected, the fault logs are updated and when all fault logs for a particular test are clear, that test can be re-run. The actual procedures for handling error correction and re-running must be administered with great care, otherwise many unnecessary abortive test shots are used.

11.7.16. System Test Library Maintenance

During system testing planning, preparation and execution, a large amount of documentation is produced. As during all other phases, it is vital that this is stored centrally and is readily available for acces. All the documentation and test output should be filed and a control system should ensure that anything removed is returned to its place.

11.7.17. Systems Testing Review and Sign-off

When all the scheduled tests have been completed successfully, the documentation should be checked to make sure that it is correct. The fault logs should be examined to ascertain that they have all been signed off. Users, operations, technical support and data administration must be asked to sign off the system testing as complete, thus formally agreeing it.

11.7.18. User Acceptance Testing

If either user testing or parallel running is to occur, this follows the same procedure as systems testing, again using fault logs to report errors. A formal sign-off must again be obtained before system implementation can begin. If the users' data was integrated into the system test, the users can accept the system without further testing, provided they satisfy themselves that the output conforms to the expected results.

11.8. SOFTWARE REQUIREMENTS

The testing processes can be considerably simplified through the use of the software tools such as: -

*   Module Testers

*   Test Data Generators

*   Interrupt Handlers

*   Coverage Monitors

*   File Comparison Utilities

*   Query Languages

If any or all of these are available, they should be taken into account in the test plan.

Module testers are pre-written modules which contain the common code normally associated with drivers/stubs to be used during top-down incremental testing. Module testers facilitate early testing of unit modules, automatic driver/stub generation and result checking, and simulate early subsystems and system level checking.

Test Data Generators automatically generate test files and document and audit this process. The file generation process is predictable, repeatable and standardised. In addition, the process may be imbedded directly in the input/output module.
Interrupt Handlers reduce the effects of "Program Control Interrupts" during complex integration tests. They also reduce trivial service interrupts and they improve testing performance and results overall.

Coverage Monitors are particularly useful during "White Box Testing" as they can determine whether every statement or decision has been tested. The major advantages of coverage monitors are that they identify "spotty" test, logic holes and unreachable code.

File Comparison Utilities facilitate the comparison of non-database files. When two similar files are compared, a report is produced which indicates the data differences. An application of this utility may be the same file at two stages of development, or conversion files compared to new files.

11.9. TESTING IN A DATABASE ENVIRONMENT

All maintenance changes should be tested and approved before they are applied to the operating system. The Data and Database Administrators should know how any change impacts all areas of the database particularly in a multi-user environment. Some maintenance changes that require complete testing are database restructuring and/or reorganisation, version and/or release control of systems software, and application software changes.

The changes made to any part of the database potentially impact the entire operation of that system; therefore the thorough testing of the procedures for testing is highly recommended as well. For the testing procedures to be effective, they should be controlled as any other application, extension, or change. The Data and Database Administrators should analyze the version and/or status of the production and test data. Backup and recovery are particularly important before any test is made to be sure that quick recovery is possible if it should be necessary.

REFERENCES

1. THE ART OF SOFTWARE TESTING, G.J. Myers, John Wiley & Sons, New York, 1979.

12. ORGANISATIONAL IMPLICATIONS CAUSED BY THE FOURTH GENERATION ENVIRONMENT

12.1 INTRODUCTION

In the three years or so that the term "4th Generation" has been used to describe a wide variety of software, various degrees of success have been achieved. Why is it that after all the hype, not every company has been successful. It is the presenter's view that this is due in the main to the way companies are structured and organised. Certain factors, such as the management of data as a corporate resource, the use of structured methods, the role of programmers, and the involvement of end-users in application development, must be considered to make the introduction of 4th Generation Software successful.

Every person involved in the system development life-cycle will be affected by the increasing level of automation and support. Some traditional data processing roles will be radically altered, while some will become obsolete. With the adoption of automated methods, the concentration of human effort will be in the planning, analysis and design stages. New skills will need to be acquired by the programmers of today if they are to adapt to the changing environment. Although the development of an organisation's major data and processing architectures may still involve large teams, much of the subsequent application systems development will be achieved by small teams or by individuals.

At the end of 1985, two of the UK's leading independent consultants had separately looked at what were the possible areas of impact of Fourth Generation Tools on an Organisation.

David Gradwell (1) felt that there were three major areas of impact on organisational requirements due to new application development tools, be they fourth generation systems or CASE Tools or whatever. The organisational structure would need to evolve to meet these new needs. He stated that the three were as follows:-

- The distinction between programmers and analysts will weaken and then disappear.

- The importance of strategic analysis is increased. Data administration will become essential. Cross project planning and cross user department planning will become essential.

- End users will need support in their use of decision support software. This will further emphasize the need for a data administration function.

Roger Tagg (2) believed that there were three areas of change needed for an organisation to successfully use fourth generation systems:-

- The demarcation lines between programmers and analysts become less valid.

- The position of data processing within the organisation will change, with the necessary change in the sort of person who is manager of the area - more a business manager.

- The involvement of end users in actually developing solutions to their own problems.

As can be seen, they agreed on only two aspects, namely the distinction between programmers and analysts, and the involvement of end-users. Since that time, the Institute of Data Processing Management have issued a report (3), which has suggested that organisations who have purchased fourth generation tools have not been successful as they expected. It is perhaps unfortunate, that no real reasons for this situation, were discussed in the report. My own feelings are that this situation is due to 2 main factors :-

- Firstly, the size of the sample of organisation who were involve in the survey, was not representative of all the products

- Secondly, and of far greater importance, the organisations had not thought about changing their methodology for developing systems, the new software and it associated new techniques, as well as catering for the new problems that the software causes.

In this chapter, I shall put forward my ideas for changes to the organisation that need to be considered to take full advantage of Fourth Generation Tools and to prepare for the coming Fifth Generation products. The areas I shall cover are as follows :-

- Application Developers
- Data Administration
- Database Administration
- Project Management
- Security Administration
- End User Involvement

12.2.   APPLICATION DEVELOPERS - NOT ANALYST OR   PROGRAMMER

Fourth generation products have been designed to shield developers from some of the major time-consuming environmental elements they have had to deal with in the past; such as operating system, JCL, TP monitor, etc. This liberates time which the developer can use in concentrating upon the organisation - the actual business problem being addressed - and improves communication between data processing and users. Figure 12.1 illustrates this point.

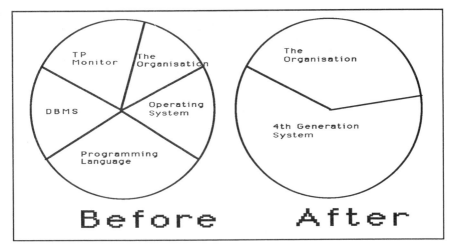

Figure 12.1 : Fourth Generation Software Impact on Developers

Fourth generation products also enable developers and end-users to develop applications much faster than with conventional languages. The developer can often create programs that have a tenth of the number of instructions that COBOL would require, and in a tenth of the time. The end-user is helped by fourth generation languages by being able to specify what he/she wants the computer to do, and not how to do it. This has led to a new problem , that of the overworked analyst.

David Gradwell at VLDB in Brighton (4) felt that fourth generation products in the main did help in the following areas :-

•   Productivity gains in program coding and testing

•   Reduction in the need to understand TP monitors and Database Management Systems

•   Easier end-user access to data

On the other hand, he saw that fourth generation tools had led to overloaded development machines as well as giving no real support to the analysis phase of the development of a system. In addition the majority of Fourth Generation products had tow major failings :-

•   No support for word processing and text management

•   Little or no version control

He went onto talk about the arrival of CASE tools, and stated his belief that there was a collision between these two sets of products. It is my belief that we need both sets of tools to be able to fully develop and maintain applications. The current way in which certain CASE tools have reverted to generate COBOL, and their rigidity in making changes, I feel is a backward step. When working for a software supplier in 1987, I found that it was their belief that you needed both sets of tools need to co-exist ,not only for ease of maintenance, but also to evolve rather than revolutionise application development .

Figure 12.2 : Fourth Generation Products - CASE Tools Clash ?

As far as systems development careers are concerned, the demand for data processing expertise will continue. End users will not want to manage large scale "production" applications themselves, and Information Centres will not be used for this purpose. However, there will be a trend for data processing professionals to specialise in a certain industry. The background of an individual in banking, insurance, or manufacturing will become more and more important as compared to experience with this or that operating system or programming language. Also, personal communication skills will become a major factor in job placement and advancement. The data processing community must learn to speak the language of the user, not expect the user to learn data processing jargon. Again, fourth generation languages have the goal of expressing a program in business terms rather than data processing terms. Using a common language will improve communication skills, we will see the ascendancy of information centre specialists. These are individuals with high communication skills who are well trained in the usage of information centre products. They serve as a resource to assist end-users in developing their own applications in the information centre.

In a combination of CASE and Fourth Generation tools, data processing will have a two-edged sword that will speed the phases of an application life-cycle. At the same time, they will radically effect the working practices, not only of developers and analysts, but also the end-user must contribute more to the analysis and design process.

12.3.   PROJECT MANAGEMENT

Without a project manager, bad systems are implemented late and over budget. Sometimes there is no doubt that this happens with a project manager, but the single most over-riding characteristics of a project manager is he/she achieves goals, reaches targets and delivers on time. Expected to manage technology, people and the change process, the project manager can face the following potential difficulties even before the development process for a new system has begun:

- dissatisfaction of users with previously developed computer-based systems;

- project management methods and organisation structures inappropriate for new systems development;

- inadequately skilled systems development staff;

- poorly developed systems planning mechanisms.

The project manager will need to be technically competent so as to choose the technical computing strategies most appropriate for the application development. He will need to be an effective planned, a good controller of his team and sensitive to the problems of implementing change. He will need to be a good manager of his team and capable of training members to discharge their duties efficiently. Part of his success will depend on the organisational relationships between himself and the rest of the organisation. It is important for the project manager to establish a firm base in the organisational hierarchy and, in particular, to be sure of his own upward reporting mechanism.

The role of the project manager can be divided into 5 components, as shown in Figure 12.3. It is likely that the project manager will need to review and constantly modify the business justification for the project.

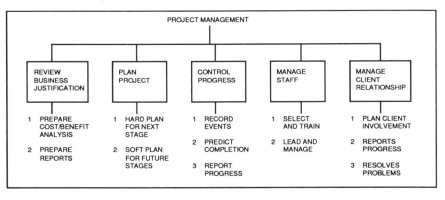

Figure 12.3: Five Components of Project Management

During the project development cycle, there is a constant need for everyone in the team to reinforce the benefits of the work being done. Short and long term plans will need to be prepared in detail, justified and costed out; and the preparation of hard plans for the next stage and soft plans for future stages will be an important part of the project manager's job. This is because there are always deviations from the plan which, when identified, will cause re-planning to be done. Controlling progress means monitoring the work of others and hence there is a need to manage staff. The project manager is also responsible for managing the relationships between the team and the client. This means many things from:

- influencing the attitudes of the client staff;

- controlling and motivating his own people to present a positive and helpful attitude towards the client;

- selling new ideas;

- reporting progress;

In a modern fourth generation environment, the notion of creating or establishing an application system and application programs is an activity, which is distinct from writing the application program. While in some organisations the same person might do both tasks, in other organisations the task of establishing applications and their assigned resources may be accomplished by an "Application Administrator", who may be a Project Leader, Data Administrator, Chief Programmer or Developer. This person determines the specific application programs which are going to be built and assigns to the specific dataviews, panels, reports and other programs. This role is a distinct role from writing the application program.

12.4. ORGANISATIONAL IMPLICATIONS OF DATA ADMINISTRATION

The positions of the Data Administrator and the Database Administrator are relatively new to data processing environments. Traditionally, their functions and responsibilities are handled by various people participating in individual projects or departments within the processing environment. However, the database environment makes it necessary to centralise control and management under one administrative group.

Data Administration, according to the British Computer Society Data Administration Working Party (DAWP) (5), will primarily have a co-ordinating role, and will otherwise play a controlling role, related to the use of data. A more active role that this should only be adopted when necessary to advise, train, or co-ordinate to achieve specific longer term goals. There are areas where guidelines need to be drawn. Outside these areas, data administration will rarely have authority or responsibility, but as general rule, inside them data administration will be involved at a level that reflects the level of existing or potential data related problems. Data administration is not responsible for actual data values of the data of the organisation, but will be concerned with the meaning of the data. A definition derived by DAWP (6) for data administration is as follows:

Data Administration is the corporate service which assists the provision of information systems by controlling and/or co-ordinating the definitions [format and characteristics] the usage of reliable and relevant data. Data that is internal to an organisation can be controlled, whilst data from external sources [eg. tax rates, independent marketing surveys] that is used by an organisation can only be co-ordinated.

Data administration is primarily concerned with problems that cross company organisational boundaries. It follows that the relationship between data administration and the organisational structure is the crux of data administration.

Data administration is as concerned with the way the company is organised as it is with the data - someone with a mathematical bent might define data administration as the intersection of data and the organisational structure.

In order to have successful data administration - that is to have good data - a company must be prepared to pay the necessary price. This price is not so much in terms of money and resources, but in terms of organisational willingness to adapt, co-operate and spend time and effort helping to set up and carry out successful data administration. There are companies where the different parts and functions are not prepared to co-operate with each other, where any issue crossing organisational boundaries is seized on purely as an opportunity for political in-fighting. There is virtually no chance of making data administration work in such companies. Attempts to set up data administration will fail, and can be of value solely in showing up this intrinsic weakness within the company.

The scope of the Data Administration function must be as wide as is needed by a particular organisation, in order to achieve the aims of cost effective use of the data of the organisation. A Data Administration function will always perform a service role, and will be involved in the identification and solution of the data aspects of the problems of the organisation. Data Administration does not directly control data, except data about the data of the organisation and data about its own function.

12.4.1. Responsibilities of Data Administration

There are a number of areas in which the Data Administrator should have responsibilities assigned to him. These breakdown into roughly 14 major task areas:

- Data Administration Policy - the establishment of the principles of data management which in their turn determine the responsibilities of Data Administration.

- Identification of Corporate Information requirements - The determination and the obtaining of acceptance of the policies for the identification of corporate requirements.

- Generating a corporate awareness of data - The education of the company of the importance of data. An awareness of the value of data as a company asset has to be created. In addition, the knowledge of what data exists and for what purpose the data is used must be communicated.

- Data Analysis - The selection of the data analysis methods in conjunction with the development of procedures for its use. Assistance with the production of business data models and the monitoring of the consistency of the results.

- Data definition - The establishment of standards for the definition of data and the medium for the recording and communication of the definitions.

- Data Dictionary control - The establishment of the requirements for procedures for data dictionary control.

- Problems related to data.

- Physical Data Models - in that Database Administration (5), provides technical support for data administration: Performing database design and development, being responsible for organising and defining the logical view of data, providing education on database technology, and providing support to users in operational database related activities.

- Impact assessment - assessing the impact of data changes.

- Data Access - The design and gaining acceptance of access authorisation rules for an organisation. The arbitration of disputes that arise from requests for access to data.

- Privacy, Security and Integrity - The implementation and the ensuring of compliance within the company of aspects of data protection legislation. The establishment of the strategy for specifying the requirements for privacy of data. The determination of the strategy should ensure that the requirements for data integrity, data security and privacy are addressed during physical systems design.

- Data Duplication - The promotion of a policy for a single source of data and the encouraging of the sharing of data across applications.

- Data Archiving - The establishment of a strategy for archiving data.

- Monitoring usage of data - Monitoring live running to ensure that the strategies for data integrity, data security and privacy are being followed. Monitoring the use and the content of the data dictionary to ensure compliance with the established rules.

The responsibilities of the Data Administrator will vary from company to company. The responsibilities will vary both in areas covered and the degree of responsibilities involved. Thus the Data Administrator may control, manage, advise, audit, plan, set standards - or any combination. It would be wrong and dangerous to try to specify a set of exact responsibilities that will suit all companies. The right set of responsibilities for the individual company will depend on the particular nature, business and history of the company. There are however, certain factors that will strongly affect the responsibilities of the Data Administrator:

- homogeneity or complexity of company structure;

- company policy on centralisation and decentralization

- use of Database Management System

- system inconsistencies

- data protection legislation

- corporate business plans

12.5. THE CHANGING ROLE OF THE DATABASE ADMINISTRATOR

The Database Administrator is primarily responsible for the technical implementation of the database environment, the day-to-day operations of the database, and the policies governing its everyday use. The Database Administrator's responsibilities include:

- Establishing technical standards and guidelines: Makes sure that all he data are defined, organised, and represented in such a way that multiple uses and applications are allowed, and that end-users, programmers, and analysts have specific, standard guidelines by which data may be input, updated or accessed.

- Supporting policies and conventions of management: Makes sure that the users maintain the policies and conventions determined by management, including the Data Administrator, governing the use and evolution of the database.

- Reviewing application system candidates: Determines whether conform to the design requirements of the database or whether they need to be modified before they are converted to the database system.

- Database design: Analyses the needs of the users on a priority basis and employs the most cost-effective techniques for the design of the database to ensure that the immediate and future requirements of the users are met effectively.

- Control of the database environment: Continues monitoring and control of the database environment after the system is in full operation, including data dictionary maintenance, system additions or extensions, and documentation.

- Technical implementation of data integrity requirements: Implements the necessary data locks and restriction, conducts periodic security audits, supervises the authorisation of access to specific data, and investigates all known security breaches to protect the integrity of the data in the database.

- Training for the database environment: Holds responsibility for the education and training of the users in the principles and policies of database use which includes making current documentation available to the users.

The Database Administrator is a clearing house, a central agency for the collection, classification, and distribution of the information and skills necessary to the success and maximum benefit of the database system.

The Database Administrator's primary functions have lain in the areas of design, control, and evolution.

12.5.1. Design

The Database Administrator designs the database to reflect the immediate needs of the users and accommodate their future needs. Some of the general responsibilities of the Database Administrator in the design of the database include the definition of the content and the organisation of the database [data structure], the definition of the access to the database [including the logical and physical reference paths and methods], and the allocation of physical storage in the database[s]. The database design not only should reflect the users' needs at the time of the design, but it should also provide the means for incremental growth throughout its life cycle to meet the future needs of the users. Therefore, the design effort is extremely important to the overall success of the database system.

There are two major impacts on the way in which this role has to evolve, namely Fourth generation tools and CASE tools. With the former, there is need to be able to adapt current physical design techniques to work with prototyping systems. To gain the maximum benefits, the underlying Database management Systems must, I believe be relational, so as to take advantage of flexibility and of ease of use. Both Applied Data Research (7) and Cincom (8) have done something in this area. The second impact form Fourth Generation Systems on design is the ability to exploit tuning possibilities effectively. This normally seems only to be possible within a fully integrated environment, ie. the database management system andfourth generation product are supplied by the same supplier. In the case of CASE tools, as they progress further down the line of first generation of physical model from conceptual model, the black art of design for a particular database management system disappears. This is the area where Expert systems are really starting to get a hold, for the vast majority of design techniques can be implemented as sets of rules. The role of the Database Administrator will therefore lessen in this area of design.

12.5.2. Control

After the database system is in full operation, the Database Administrator initiates control techniques to assure the consistent and effective performance of the system.

Through testing and acceptance procedures, the Database Administrator is satisfied that the design of the database is fulfilling the immediate requirements of the system, and that it is evolving properly to conform to the future requirements of the system. By monitoring the inputs and outputs of data through edit and validation rules, data checking, and access controls, the Database Administrator identifies any inconsistencies in data integrity.

The Database Administrator also reviews all existing application systems for their consistency with the data definition and usage standards, so the systems can be effectively converted to the database environment without major revisions. The Database Administrator makes sure that the development of new application systems effectively meet the users' requirements as well. The Database Administrator monitors the use of the database through access statistics and request/response statistics to assure the maximum efficiency of the system.

In this area, once again Database Management System suppliers are working to automate the tuning process, through the use of Expert system technology.

12.5.3. Evolution

The Database Administrator determines the specifications and design of the extensions, services, and utilities for the database environment. The Database Administrator also documents the evolution of the environment via the data dictionary. The Database Administrator maintains the system development life cycle and the procedures for security, privacy, integrity, and recovery. This helps to assure that the system remains effective in meeting both the current and future needs of the users.

This role is still needed . It is very difficult to envisaged there being no human involvement in the sort of tasks described.

12.6. SECURITY ADMINISTRATION

The issues of privacy, security and integrity within the database environment are important in database design, performance and maintenance. Privacy, security and integrity are all closely related concepts, but, in fact, the differences among the three are substantial. The specific definition of each of the concepts are as follows:

Privacy   the right of individuals or institutions to control the collection and dissemination of personal information

Security   the protection of the computer resources from accidental or intentional destruction, modification, or disclosure

Integrity   the correctness, accuracy, and timeliness of data within a certain level of appropriateness

The Data Administrator and the Database Administrator are responsible for the privacy, security, and integrity within the database environment including all data and processing. Security of the database includes the protection of data from deliberate or inadvertent disclosure, modification or destruction. System integrity is the consistency, completeness, adherence to specifications, freedom from intrusion, and predictability of a system.

12.6.1. Computer Security Issues

One might ask at this point, "Why do we need security?" The answer is not a simple one. One of the primary reasons is the growing realisation that data is an asset of a company. Because computer professionals have done such a good job of establishing computer resources in the business environment, many businesses today would not survive beyond a week to ten days if they could not process their data. For example, imagine how long a bank or department store would stay in business without its computerised data of the ability to process it.

Many years ago when data processing was a purely 'batch' process, security and control were implemented through external, physical measures. The exposure was low because much of a company's vital information was not stored on the computer. As data processing has matured, almost all of a company's data has moved to the computer. Storage of all records on computers means that highly sensitive information about company planning strategies or personnel is now stored electronically rather than in someone's locked filing cabinet.

As we make advances in computing technology, the exposures associated with potential loss of integrity in our computing environment also increases. The development of large shared databases, increased ability to access this data online, and the proliferation of remote terminals is no longer restricted to computing professionals. For instance, consider the growth of Automated Teller Machines, Point of Sale Terminals, grocery checkout scanners and the increased use of electronic transfer of funds, all of which have directly affected the general public.

Of course, this increased impact of computers on the general public has also enhanced public awareness of security issues. The public is rapidly becoming aware that the data is now owned by the bank or the credit service bureau, but that the data is really theirs. So the need for accuracy and integrity of data is coming closer to home for the general public. Anyone who has ever had a personal loan request refused because of information supplied by one of the many credit agencies has certainly felt the impact of the need for data accuracy.

Another item of increased public awareness is the publication from time to time of incidents of the use of computers to perpetrate fraud or embezzle money. While only the largest cases receive widespread notoriety, each insurance funding scandal or misappropriation of funds through the misuse of computers plans yet another seed of doubt in the mind of the public.

The last and perhaps most important incentive for the establishment of computing security is the increased interest by legislative bodies in accounting controls and individual privacy. Legislation is now in force in the following countries:

- USA
- France
- West Germany
- Sweden
- Canada
- United Kingdom

12.6.2. What to Secure?

What we have to ask ourselves is what should we be protecting:-

- Is it the data itself?

- Is it access to the data?

- Is it access to the physical storage devices on which the data is stored?

- Or is it some combination of the above?

To answer this question we must look at the objectives of Security Administration which are as follows:-

- To implement the Security Policy of your organisation, using the security facilities that are available on the market place that are the most cost effective.

- To maintain the security details appertaining to your organisation.

Therefore Security in my view, should be based on data and data content, and not on storage device and terminal access. What sort of facilities have you available in your fourth generation environment? Well beside OEM access control packages, such as RACF and ACF II, certain fourth generation products have facilities in built in them to protect the data of your organisation and access to it. This is normally implemented by the use of facilities in the underlying dictionary and/or database management system.

12.7. END USER INVOLVEMENT AND SUPPORT

The watchword of the Eighties and the Nineties is user involvement. The end user will be involved in every aspect of data processing, including design, development and testing. Singer (9) states that the demand for this involvement has come from factors which operated in the late Sixties and the Seventies :-

- A strong feeling that data processing technology was so complicated that account-ants, managers, etc. could not possibly understand it. As a result, organisations consistently found that computer systems did not meet the basic needs of the users.

- The rising cost of complicated systems was another factor. the time taken to develop systems is longer, and in addition requires more people to work on it. The hardware cost per CPU cycle may have dropped, but the cost in development time has risen dramatically.

- The consideration of purchased software packages as being a valid alternative to in-house development, is a third factor. the selection of a good package requires experts not only from data processing but also from the end user groups.

- The growing awareness of end users that the data they need to perform their jobs can be obtained from the computer.

If the trend towards direct user involvement is to be successful, data processing managers should take the lead in developing a planned, realistic approach to working with end users, Too often a combined team of data processing personnel and end users will sit round a table with all the co-operation of two nine-year-old boys fighting over a cricket bat! In the Eighties and Nineties, such un-businesslike behaviour cannot be tolerated. The stakes of economical survival and profitability are now too high to allow individuals or groups to play ego games inside an organisation.. data processing managers are in a perfect position to break the cycle of disagreement and mistrust which seems to developed whenever their staff and the end users get together. Several very simple steps have been suggested by Singer (9) to help insure that such a team approach can be achieved :-

- Non technical users must be educate in basic data processing concepts, such as disk versus tape operations, database as opposed to conventional files, and in-house development versus purchased packages. The nature of the educational process will depend on the situation and circumstances of the organisation and the specific project.

- Verify that all data processing staff involved an a design project with users have a basic understanding of the application in question. Just as many data processing managers are surprised by the lack of basic computer knowledge of users, user management are equally surprised at the lack of communication caused by data processing staff who have absolutely no idea what users are talking about.

• Once both data processing and users have been cross-trained to some degree, data processing managers can then take the lead by planning the entire task around a formalised project management approach. The degree of formalisation will depend on the length. the complexity, and the importance of the task or project in question.

Besides user involvement in the development of their own systems, there is another significant trend in recent years, namely the Information Centre. The function of an Information Centre is to encourage, train, and support end users to develop applications themselves. With help, end users can generate a wide variety of applications including data query, data input and editing, report generation, decision-support systems, and many classes of application programs. The traditional data processing systems life cycle is thus bypassed, which gives users results much faster, but at a cost of their own time. In theory, developers are then free to concentrate on systems without having to shift priorities to accommodate an end-user's ad hoc requests.

Information Centres utilize a wide variety of languages and tools. usually these facilities include general purpose tools such as query languages, report generators, graphic generators, decision support systems, and application generators. Additional specialised tools may also be used for financial planning, statistical analysis, project management, text processing, desk-top publishing, and computer-aided design. It is important to note in regard to this area that although the software tools get most of the spotlight, they still need to operate upon data. The data has to be stored and managed somehow, usually by a database management system. The choice of database management system will actually set limits upon what end users can and cannot do with those friendly software tools. Two distinct schools of thought on this subject have evolved, namely the "truth database approach" and the "dual database approach". The dual database approach mandates that redundancy between operational systems and decision support systems is a valid approach. Examples of database management systems that support this are IBM's DB2 and IMS, FOCUS,and ICL's IDMS with INGRES. The truth database approach dictates that there will be one and only one copy of the database for all users. Examples of database management systems that support this approach are Applied Data Research's DATACOM/DB, Cincom's TIS/XA and Cullinet's IDMS/R.

The Information Centre has not only had to tackle this software problem of which approach to adopt, but also has fallen into the mistake of "empire building" in a number of instances. The Information Centre should provide assistance to the end users to develop their own solutions and not to do the work itself. The one main exception to this rule would be in the case of board level management. Here the best way that I have heard of was describe by David Owen of ICL Asia Pacific Pty Limited at Malayasian National Computer Conference (10). Each Senior Executive had a computer expert as an assistant. This person provided the technical knowledge and wisdom to be able to extract the required information using the best possible software tool in the quickest possible manner. In the paper he described how these consultants were used to help the executives put together the organisation's yearly plan, whereas it used to take some 3 months to do this , it was now possible to do this in 3 weeks.Here we have a fine example of effective use of data processing people with good knowledge of a business area, providing effective and efficient service to the end users.

Perhaps the greatest danger of Information Centre operation, or of the spread of small computers and user-friendly software, is that multiple, uncoordinated data structures will be used. The answer to this is well-controlled data administration.

12.8. CONCLUSIONS

If we are to effectively use Fourth Generation tools, we must be prepared to evolve our organisational structures. The role of data processing is changing rapidly and the needs of our end users are changing even more and even faster. With the realisation amongst senior user management, that to survive in business in the Eighties and the Nineties, they will need to be able to tap the Information Resource more effectively and to control it, we in data processing have to be able to respond quickly and effectively. This is not possible with :-

- the use of Third Generation Languages;

- the use of Third Generation methodologies, such as SSADM and Information Engineering in their current form;

- the rigidity of the current data processing organisation, as shown in figure 12.4;

- the demarcation line and in-fighting between end users and data processing.

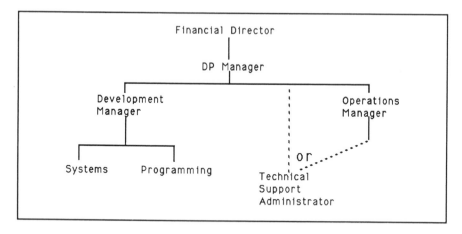

Figure 12.4 : Traditional Data Processing Department Structure

How can we tackle this? What is it we must do?

Fourth Generation Languages in themselves are not the answer. A new language will only help in the coding and testing phases of an application's life cycle. We need to be able to assist the analysis and design phases much more to produce the goods for our end users. The adoption of prototyping techniques, has certainly, where done in a controlled way, proved to be of assistance in the design phase. The CCTA have already started to adapt SSADM to use prototyping and to work more effectively with certain Fourth Generation Tools [11]. LBMS and CACI have also started to adapt their methodologies to use prototyping.

The currently available methodologies are very paper oriented. David Gradwell [4] has spoken of them not only building paper mountains but of building paper mountain ranges!

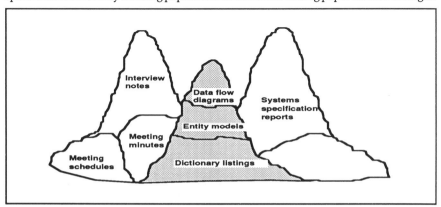

Figure 12.5 : Paper Mountain Ranges

It is here that CASE tools will assist with the automation of documentation and graphics. They will also provide the means of tackling the "analyst overload". We must be prepared to adopt a methodology that suits our organisation, as well as being able to work with our current software and hardware. To take advantage of fourth generation technology the methodology we choose must support not only prototyping but also structured analysis and design. The methodology must be flexible, so that new techniques can replace old ones without a complete redo of the methodology. This is only possible if the methodology is based on a framework approach, as advocated by the British Computer Society Database Specialist Group's Information Systems Analysis and Design (ISAD) working party in their Journal of Development (12).

The structure of data processing must evolve to take account of the changes in demand upon its service, and the changes in technology. Too often I have seen as a consultant organisations, whose structure is based upon technology of the late Sixties, with the power base in the wrong hands. In addition data processing managers are themselves to blame for their lack of knowledge of new software and techniques. They have not spent time on keeping abreast of our changing world. We must understand the importance of data as a resource to our organisations, and give power within data processing , if not within the organisation to the administration of this resource. I have in a forthcoming book looked at ways that Data Administration can be evolved in an organisation to get to the right level [13]. But it is not just data administration that is important. Development of systems has changed dramatically, thanks in the main to Fourth Generation technology and to adoption of methodologies. The use of teams of coders, designers, analysts and end users has proved effective when all the right planning has been done up front.

What sort of organisation should we being aiming for then? In figure 12.6, I show what I believe should be our goal.

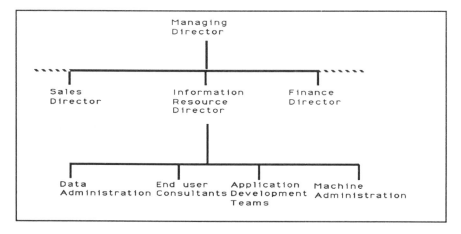

Figure 12.6 : Data Processing - The Future structure ?

The probable outcome of the latest Fifth Generation work will be to strengthen communications between users and developers. This communication will not be confined as at present to the specification document, but will use computer graphics facilities, as seen in current CASE tools and prototyping techniques. If the prototype is to be easily converted for the software needed.

The use of fourth generation systems and CASE tools will remove the current bottleneck of systems development, but only if data processing itself recognises that it must reorganise itself. In addition we must realise that software tools on their own will not help . Neither will methodologies on their own solve the problem. It is the combination of the tools and the techniques with the right organisation.

The potential for new methods and machines and software within an intelligent workbench, falls under the heading of "knowledge transfer". This includes not only the initial capture of knowledge during analysis, but also all mapping activities, such as physical database design. In each case , the rules governing the activity will be defined and used in a rule-based expert system , to support and automate a given function in the application life cycle. These principles of knowledge engineering and artificial intelligence, combined with the use of models of the business and prototyping will allow the users of computer systems to become more completely involved in their creation. Computer systems will become an extension of the business, with the creation of new systems and maintenance of existing systems being triggered solely by changes in the business environment.

REFERENCES

1.   APPLICATION GENERATORS FOR IMPROVED PRODUCTIVITY, D.J.L.Gradwell, How to manage The Information Resource, Edited by S.Holloway, British Computer Society Database Specialist Group, 1985.

2.   ORGANISATIONAL ENVIRONMENT OF SUCCESSFUL USE OF 4GLS AND AGS, R..Tagg, Fourth Generation Languages and Application Generators, edited by D.Martland, S.Holloway and L.Bhabuta, The Technical Press - Unicom Applied Information Technology Report Series, 1986.

3.   4GL REPORT, VOLUME 1 A SURVEY OF BEST PRACTICE, Institute of Data Processing Managers,1986

4.   ANALYST/DESIGNER WORKBENCHES, D.J.L.Gradwell, 13th VLDB Conference, Brighton, September 1987

5.   DATA ADMINISTRATION : A MANAGER'S GUIDE, British Computer Society Data Administration Working Party, 1987.

6   INTERNAL PAPER OF BRITISH COMPUTER SOCIETY DATA ADMINISTRATION WORKING PARTY 1982.

7   METHODOLOGY SALES PACK, Applied Data Research UK Ltd., 1987

8   TIS/XA MANTIS SALES BROCHURE, MAN-003-25M-8604-TH&W, Cincom

9.   THE DATA PROCESSING MANAGER'S SURVIVAL MANUAL [A GUIDE FOR MANAGING PEOPLE AND RESOURCES], L.M.Singer, John Wiley and Sons, 1982.

10. PRACTICAL BENEFITS OF EXECUTIVE DECISION SUPPORT SYSTEMS, David Owen and Mark C.Volpato,Proceedings of the Malayasian National Computer Conference, Kuala Lumper, Malaysia, November 1985

11. SSADM IMPLENTATION (QuichBuild), Information Systems Engineering Report, Information Technology in the Civil Service, CCTA, Draft for development, January 1987

12.   INFORMATION SYSTEMS DEVELOPMENT : A FLEXIBLE FRAMEWORK, Journal of Development, Information Systems Analysis and Design Working Party, British Computer Society Database Specialist Group, editor R.Maddison, 1983-84

13.   DATA ADMINISTRATION, Simon Holloway, Gower Technical Press, 1988

FURTHER READING

- The State of Practice of Data Administration, M.L.Gillinson, Comm. ACM, vol 25, Oct 1982.

- The Database Administrator, J.K.Lyon, Wiley, 1976.

- Data Base Administration, J.L.Weldon, Plenum Press, 1981.

- Information Systems and Organisational Change, P.G.W.Keen, Comm. ACM, vol 24, no 1, pp24-33, Jan 1981.

APPENDIX A
Methodology Phases and their Deliverables

METHODOLOGY PHASES	DELIVERABLES

1.0 Business Planning
1. Mission Statements
   Enterprise wide
   By Product Line
   By Organization
2. Business Goals
3. Critical Success Factors
4. Environmental Factors
5. Objectives

2.0 Information Resource Planning

2.1 Develop/Adopt Change Control Procedures
1. Change Control Procedures

2.2 Develop/Adopt Data Admin. Standards/Procedures
1. Data Adm. Stds. & Procedures

2.3 Define Business Objectives/ Organization & Major Functions
1. Organization Chart
2. Function Chart
3. List of Objectives -Prioritized & Weighted
4. Process, Organization, Function Descriptions
5. Responsibility Matrix (Proc., Func., Org., Obj.)

2.4 Document Current Info. Systems
1. List of Current Systems & Major Programs
2. Process/Function v/s System/ Program Matrix
3. Info. about Systems: Age, Architecture, Location, Cost of Maintenance, etc.
4. Problems with current Systems
5. System/Entity Create/Use Matrix
6. Enhancement Needs Backlog Prioritized
7. Inventory of Information Systems Resources: People, Capabilities, Hardware, Software, etc.

2.5 Identify Major Business Entities
1. High Level Entity List
2. Entity-Relationship Charts
3. Entity Creation/Use Matrix
4. High Level Subject Areas

METHODOLOGY PHASES	DELIVERABLES
2.6 Develop High Level Info Systems Architecture for Hardware, Software,Applications and Geographic	1 Prioritized Applications 2. Subject Data Base/Application Schema 3. Applications Architecture 4 Geographic Architecture 5 Software Architecture 6 Hardware Architecture
2.7 Develop Implementation Plan for Hardware, Software,& Organization	1. Information Systems Plan -Application Development Plan -Plans & Strategies for DP 2 Project Definition for HighPriority Projects: Scope Project Data Model Work Plans

3.0 Functions & Data Specification

3.1 Identify Functional Require- -ments	1 Description of all Functions and Processes 2 Input/Output Descriptions (User views). 3 Procedural Flows 4 Security & Control needs. 5. Data Flow Diagrams 6 Function Decomposition Diagrams
3.2 Determine Current Systems Support	1 Detailed list of Current Systems support- ing Processes within Project Scope 2 Systems/Procedures for Migration 3 Current System Data Models 4 System Software used in Current Systems. 5 Data Migration Issues 6 List of Pros & Cons about Migration Software Tools
3.3 Develop Preliminary Data Models	1 List of Entities 2 Entity-Association Charts 3 First cut specs. for Entity, Associations, Integrity Constraints, Rules (mainly from User-views) 4 Synthesis report with high level Subject Areas
3.4 Select Implementation Tools and Techniques	1 Detailed explanation for choice of Tools and software:

METHODOLOGY PHASES	DELIVERABLES

3.5 Develop Plan & Review Project   1 Project Development Plans and
     Development Strategy   Strategy

4.0 Application Software Acquisition & Design

4.1 Develop Selection Criteria
1 List of Functional Reqmts.
2 List of Data Requirements
3 User Flexibility Areas Desired
4 Hardware/Software Capability and
   Compatibility
5 Service/Software Support Criteria

4.2 Acquire, Evaluate & Test
1 Request for purchase/tender
2 Evaluation Results
3 Test Results
4 Recommendations

4.3 Plan Integration & Install
1 Migration/Installation Plans
2 Data Integration with Corporate Model

5.0 Iterative System Requirements Development

5.1 Define User System Specs.
     Formats & Processing
1 Sample Transaction Screens
2. Sample Reports Formats
3. Rules enforced in Processing Transactions/
   Reports Processing, Security,etc.
4 Volume information
5 Requirements for response time
6. Transaction/Report v/s Data Matrix :
   Use, Create, Update, Delete, etc.
7 Distributed Processing Requirements.

5.2 Perform Detailed Data Analysis
1 Detailed Data Definition Reports
2 Entity/Association for Transactions/
   Reports
3 Synthesis of Project Model
4 Entity-Association Charts
5 Integrity Constraints for Data and
   Associations

5.3 Determine Preliminary
     Processing Logic Maps
1 Processing Logic for Transactions/
   Reports (5.1)
2. Preliminary Logical Access

METHODOLOGY PHASES	DELIVERABLES
5.4 Generate/Write Prototype Programs	1 Programs Generated in this Phase 2 Programs developed for the Prototype
5.5 Develop and Test System Prototype	1 System Details: -Menu's, Program links, Test DB details 2. Test Data (Example DB) 3 Test Results 4 List of Procedures/Programs not prototyped including reasons.
5.6 Develop Preliminary Project Technical Architecture	1 Architecture Report for Hardware, Software, and Applications: eg. CICS, VTAM, etc.. Rough Programming Units How it fits with overall Architecture defined in 2.6

6.0 User Procedure Formation

6.1 Develop Manual/Automated Procedures,	1 Work Flow Procedures : special attention to Manual/automated procedures. Include all Transactions & Reports. 2 Manual Back-up Procedures for computer down-time/failure 3 Exception Handling Procedures
6.2 Develop User Manuals & Training Materials	1 User Manuals 2 Training Materials

7.0 Optimize Technical Design

7.1 Develop Detailed Technical Architecture	1. More details of 5.6 2 Interfaces to other Systems. 3 Security 4 Back-up Recovery, Catastrophe Plans 5 Generated/Prototype Programs to be used in Final System
7.2 Optimize Design of Program Work Units	1 Module Design 2 Incorporate Prototype and Generated Programs 3 Structure Charts(if necessary)

METHODOLOGY PHASES	DELIVERABLES
7.3 Complete Programming Specs. & Set upTest Data (Only for Programs not Prototyped)	1 Module Specs. Including Processing Logic (from 5.0) 2 Test Data for Unit Test
7.4 Conduct Data Stability Analysis	1 Synthesized Data Model with Long Term Effects seen in Business Model 2 Highlight Differences 3 Updated Volume/Frequency Information
7.5 Complete Logical Database Design Data Model	1 Logical Access Maps 2. Fully Normalized Project 3. List of Keys (including Foreign Keys) with Logical Records.
7.6 Complete Data Distribution Design	1 Network Design 2. Horizontal/Vertical Partitioning of Data 3. Response time simulations 4 Back-up Recovery Considerations
7.7 Develop New Business/Project Conceptual Data Model	1 Complete Business & Project Models: -Data, Relationships, Constraints.
7.8 Complete Physical Database Design	1 Complete Data Dictionary Entries. 2 Simulation Results for Response Time, Efficiency 3 Distributed Physical Database Location Report
8.0 Conversion System Development	1 Conversion Plan 2 Old Systems Data Mapped to New System Data 3 Coexistence Design 4 List of Files to be Converted 5 Conversion Model test Results
9.0 Coding & Testing	
9.1 Program & Unit Test	1 Programs 2 Test Results
9.2 Implement Physical Database & Test	1 Physical DB Layout Reports 2 Test Results

METHODOLOGY PHASES	DELIVERABLES

10.0 System Test

10.1 Perform Integration Test	1 Test Plan 2 Test Results 3 Changes Made
10.2 Revise/Update User Procedures	1 Updated User Procedures
10.3 Revise/Update Programming. Specifications	1 Updated Program Specs.
10.4 Revise/Update Physical Database Model	1 Revised Physical Database Model

11.0 Convert to New System

11.1 Run Parallel Processing	1 Test Results 2 Changes made
11.2 Complete Conversion to New System	1. Updates to all Models

12.0 Production Systems Control

13.0 Systems Maintenance

APPENDIX B
Methodology Phases
and Users

PR-Prime Responsibility
P -Participating Resp
C -Consulting When Necessary
H -Helping Responsibility

Column headings (read vertically):

| MGT | END USER | SYS ANAL | DATA ANAL | DB DESNR | PROG | DA | DBA | SYS MGT | DIST MGT | HARDWARE | QA | AUDITOR |

METHODOLOGY PHASES

Phase	MGT	END USER	SYS ANAL	DATA ANAL	DB DESNR	PROG	DA	DBA	SYS MGT	DIST MGT	HARDWARE	QA	AUDITOR
1.0 Business Planning	PR						C		C				
2.0 Information Resource Planning													
2.1 Develop/Adopt Change Control Procedures		C	P	P	P	P	PR	P	PR	P	C	P	P
2.2 Develop/Adopt Data Admin. Standards/ Procedures		C	P	P	P	C	PR	P	P	P		P	P
2.3 Define Business Objectives/ Organization & Major Functions	P	PR	H	H			P		C			C	
2.4 Document Current Info. Systems & Support	P	PR	P	C	C	P	P	P	P				
2.5 Identify Major Business Entities		PR	H	H			P					C	
2.6 Develop High Level Info. Systems, Architecture - Hardware, Software, Applications, Geographic	P	P	P	H			PR	P	P	P	C	C	C
2.7 Develop Implementation plan	P	PR	P	H			P	P	P	P	P	C	P

	1	2	3	4	5	6	7	8	9	10	11	12	13
PR-Prime Responsibility	M	E	S	D	D	P	D	D	S	D	H	Q	A
P -Participating Resp	G	N	Y	A	B	R	A	B	Y	I	A	A	U
C -Consulting When Necessary	T	D	S	T		O		A	S	S	R		D
H -Helping Responsibility				D	G					T	D		I
	U	A	A	E					M	W			T
	S	N	N	S					G	M			O
	E	A	A	N					T	G			R
	R	L	L	R					T	E			

3.0 Functions & Data Specification

	1	2	3	4	5	6	7	8	9	10	11	12	13
3.1 Identify Functional Requirements	C	P	PR	P			C					C	C
3.2 Determine Current Systems Support		C	PR	P	P	P	P	P	P	P	C	C	
3.3 Develop Preliminary Data Models		P	P	PR			C				C		
3.4 Select Implementation Tools and Techniques	C	C	P	P	P	P	PR	P	P	P	C	C	C
3.5 Develop Plan & Review Project Development Strategy	C	P	P	P	C	C	P	P	PR	P	C	C	

4.0 Application Software Acquisition & Design

	1	2	3	4	5	6	7	8	9	10	11	12	13
4.1 Develop Selection Criteria	C	P	PR	P	P		P	P	P	C		C	C
4.2 Acquire, Evaluate & Test	C	C	P	P	P		P	P	PR	C		C	C
4.3 Plan Integration & Install		P	PR	P	P	P	C	C	P	C		C	

5.0 Iterative System Requirements Development

	1	2	3	4	5	6	7	8	9	10	11	12	13
5.1 Define User System Specs. - Formats & Processing		P	PR	P			C		C		C		
5.2 Perform Detailed Data Analysis		P	P	PR			C		C		C		
5.3 Determine Preliminary Processing Logic		P	PR	P							C		

```
PR-Prime Responsibility         M E S D D P D D S D H Q A
P -Participating Resp           G N Y A B R A B Y I A A U
C -Consulting When Necessary    T D S T   O   A S S R   D
H -Helping Responsibility             D G       T D   I
                                U A A E       M   W   T
                                S N N S       G M A   O
                                E A A N       T G R   R
                                R L L R         T E
```

5.0 Iterative System Requirements Development (continued)

Task													
5.4 Generate/Write Prototype Programs	C	PR	P	C	P					C			
5.5 Develop and Test System Prototype	P	PR	P	P	P	C	C	C	C		C	C	
5.6 Develop Preliminary Project Technical Architecture	C	P	P				PR	P	PR	P	C	C	

6.0 User Procedure Formation

Task													
6.1 Develop Manual/ Automated Procedures	P	PR	C								C	C	
6.2 Develop User Manuals & Training Materials	P	PR	C								C	C	

7.0 Optimize Technical Design

Task													
7.1 Develop Detailed Technical Architecture		PR	P	C	C	C	C	C	C	C			
7.2 Optimize Design of Programming Work Units		P	C	C	PR								
7.3 Complete Programming Specs. & Set up Test Data		PR	P	C	P						P	P	
7.4 Conduct Data Stability Analysis	P	P	PR			P		P					
7.5 Complete Logical Database Design		P	PR	C	C			C		C			
```
```

Responsibility legend and column headings (letters read top-to-bottom):

```
PR-Prime Responsibility        M E S D D P D D S D H Q A
P -Participating Resp          G N Y A B R A B Y I A A U
C -Consulting When Necessary   T D S T   O   A S S R   D
H -Helping Responsibility              D G         T D   I
                               U A A E         M W     T
                               S N N S         G M A   O
                               E A A N         T G R   R
                               R L L R           T E
```

7.0 Optimize Technical Design (continued)

Activity	MGTUSER	ENDANAL	SYSANAL	DATESNR	DBD	PROG	DA	DBA	SYS	DISTMGTT	HARDWMGE	QAAR	AUDITOR
7.6 Complete Data Distribution Design	P	PR	C			P	C		P			C	C
7.7 Develop New Business (& Project) Conceptual Data Model	C	P	PR			C			C			C	C
7.8 Complete Physical Data Base Design		C	P	PR	C	C	P	C	P			C	
8.0 Conversion System Development	C	PR	P	C	P	C	C	C	C	C	C	P	
9.0 Coding & Testing													
9.1 Program & Unit Test			C	C	C	PR	C	C	C		C		
9.2 Implement Physical Database & Test			C	C	PR	C		P				P	C
10.0 System Test													
10.1 Perform Integration Test	P	PR	P	P	P	C	C	C	P			P	C
10.2 Revise/Update User Procedures	P	PR	C										
10.3 Revise/Update Programming Specs.		P				PR					P		
10.4 Revise/Update Physical Database Model			P	PR				C		P	P		

PR-Prime Responsibility
P -Participating Resp
C -Consulting When Necessary
H -Helping Responsibility

	MGT	END USER	SYS ANAL	DATA ANAL	DB DESGNR	PROG	DA	DBA	SYS MGT	DIST MGT	HARDWARE	QA	AUDITOR
11.0 Convert to New System													
11.1 Run Parallel Processing	P	PR	P									P	P
11.2 Complete Conversion to New System	P	PR	P	C		C	C	C	C	C	P		
12.0 Production Systems Control	C	H		H	H		P				C	C	C
13.0 Systems Maintenance	P	P	H	P	P	H	C	PR	H	H	C	H	

INDEX